ANCHORED
IN BIAS

Fired Over "White Tears"

A Journalist's Mission to Challenge the System

LISA BENSON

Foreword by Ruby Hamad, author of *White Tears Brown Scars*

PAGE PUBLISHING, INC.
Conneaut Lake, PA

First originally published by Page Publishing 2020

ISBN 978-1-6624-0210-4 (pbk)
ISBN 978-1-6624-0211-1 (digital)

Printed in the United States of America

For my husband Carl Cooper, sisters, and true friends who constantly encourage me to speak truth to power.

CONTENTS

Foreword by Ruby Hamad 7

Introduction 9

1   In the Beginning...12

2   Kansas City, Here I Come! 19

3   Opportunities for Growth? 26

4   EEOC Complaint/Lawsuit Filed 31

5   Retaliation Continues...36

6   Unemployed and Offended 42

7   Trial Preparations...51

8   Trial Begins..57

9   Week Two of Trial...145

10   The Verdict..177

Conclusion 182

Acknowledgment..184

About the Author 186

FOREWORD

At the Cannes Film Festival in 2018, an interviewer asked actress Salma Hayek about Harvey Weinstein's decision to respond to and strenuously deny the sexual assault allegations she and fellow star Lupita Nyong'o had made against him. Weinstein had been accused by many high-profile actresses in Hollywood, most of them white, but had not responded to any of the others. "We are the easiest to get discredited," Hayek said. "It's a well-known fact. So he went back attacking the two women of color in the hopes he could discredit us."

This is a truth whose time has well and truly come. Women of color have for far too long been treated as unreliable witnesses to their own lives. Our words carry less weight, our talents go largely unrecognized, and our worth devalued. What we do seems to attract more than anyone else, derision and retaliation whenever we attempt to assert ourselves or to draw attention to how society still excludes and marginalizes us.

Lisa Benson learned this the hard way. After years of belief in the American dream, working hard, chasing after those elusive promotions, only to see those with less experience, qualifications, and proven track record race ahead of her. Benson had to admit the truth to herself: she was being held, not only because she is black and because she is a woman but because she is a black woman. Can anyone with a straight face deny that an Emmy Award-winning journalist isn't good enough at her job to warrant a small promotion in some fourteen years working at the same media organization?

Anchored in Bias gives a crucial insight into the subtle, almost imperceptible ways that systemic racism mars and limits the lives of women of color. Benson traces her early hopes and dreams for a long and rewarding career as a television journalist, only to see them dashed at every turn through no fault of her own. And though these dreams are shattered, she picks up enough pieces to provide us

7

with a blow-by-blow account of the racial discrimination lawsuit she brought against her former employer—a suit that had both a sadly predictable and pleasantly surprising outcome. Her detailed descriptions of the case make for fascinating reading in themselves, but it is in illuminating the subtle swipes, degradations, and humiliations society metes out to women of color on the daily that this book really shines.

Benson reveals without a shadow of a doubt how demoralizing it is to work your hardest, knowing your best matches those around you, and to still be regarded as lesser than, not because of how hard or well you work, but because of who you are. Women of color will no doubt see themselves in the interactions Lisa describes, where a simple disagreement with a supervisor results in accusations of being aggressive, where the mistakes of others somehow became her sole responsibility, and where no matter what she has managed to achieve—including winning an Emmy—she is told again and again that somehow, she still isn't good enough to advance in her career. After a while, these and other rejections happen too often to be a coincidence.

Anchored in Bias is a necessary insight into the machinations that work tirelessly to grind down women of color. It is a call for acceptance and understanding; it is a demand for change. But most importantly of all, it is a reminder to black women and all women of color that they are not alone, they are not imagining these things, and they are not unworthy.

Ruby Hamad
Author of "White Tears" article and book
entitled *White Tears Brown Scars*

INTRODUCTION

America is false to the past, false to the present, and solemnly binds herself to be false to the future.

—Frederick Douglass

In 2018, the way I saw my world and the people in it changed after my twenty-year career as a television news reporter/anchor came to an abrupt end. More than two decades of making slot under grueling deadlines, endless hours of breaking news coverage, and my dedication to a career I had loved since childhood all down the drain for an article I didn't even write, entitled, "How White Women Use Strategic Tears to Avoid Accountability."

I'd be lying if I said I wasn't disappointed in my fellow female coworkers who used their white-skin advantage to punish me for reading an article about systemic racism while daring to fight a race discrimination lawsuit against my employer—a lawsuit that I filed after being denied the same opportunities for growth they enjoyed as an anchor and investigative reporter.

Both of my white female coworkers told the jurors that at one point, we were "friends" at work, but neither could pinpoint the breakup. The point in which both parties acknowledged the relationship was over. That's because the relationship didn't end; it took an uncomfortable turn as I pursued my race discrimination lawsuit against the company, daring to publicly state that I deserved the same opportunities that my white-skinned colleagues enjoyed. Unbeknownst to me and steeped in their own internalized racial superiority, my lawsuit bothered them. It became clear that the current racial dynamic at the station was comfortable for them, and racial equality wasn't quite their idea of a comfortable working environment. In the years leading to the trial, both women initiated conversations about my grievances against the station and tried to patronize my journey by assuring me that they too were, at times, devalued in the workplace. The main anchor at one point even confided in me that she feared that her age and size was becoming an issue for top management. But while they tried to silence my voice and trivialize my grievances, I had to remind both women on separate occasions that they were given opportunities at the company that I had not been given in more than a decade of me being employed. The lack of promotion for me didn't seem to bother them, but the fact that I was still on the weekends struck a nerve somehow with both women. Not enough for either to be an advocate or an ally for me in front of our superiors, just enough to conjure up a brief sigh and a head tilt before going on with their day.

The opportunity to get rid of the black woman, who was a constant reminder of their white privilege, came in the form of an article on Theguardian.com website. I had the nerve to not only read the article entitled, "How White Women Use Strategic Tears to Avoid Accountability" but also share it on my personal Facebook page, which, ironically, was set to private.

Initially, I did not understand the personal offense my coworkers took in me merely reading and sharing an article about the racial dynamic that can exist between white women and women of color. My pure ignorance and curiosity forced me to dig in and figure it out. Through lots of anti-racism books, forums, workshops, and my diversity and inclusion studies through Cornell University, I realized the mere topic of race was stressful for white people. Period. Part of their problem with the article was the fact that it generalized white people, when so much of their identity is founded in individualism and meritocracy. In fact, while on the stand, both women accused me of categorizing white women in a negative light, omitting the fact that I did not author the article. Through my studies and watching my trial play out in court, it became clear that white people like to claim that all their opportunities are earned and have nothing to do with the fact that they are white. As much as they like to deny it, life has clearly taught them that their race is an automatic qualification for fair treatment and opportunities. Whereas, as a black woman, I was raised to understand that I have to work extra hard to qualify to be seen as more than just my skin color. From driving down the street to applying for a job, my race has always been a factor.

Through my two-week trial, it became clear that my racial discrimination lawsuit, coupled with this article about interpersonal race relations, was a stress point for the six-figure main anchor who had nothing to do with my grievance, and the former nurse turned investigative reporter who got the position I applied for. This article and my lawsuit forced these two white women to see themselves in the dynamic of race. Something they probably didn't have to do in their normal everyday lives. And who am I to make them stop, think, and even see an article about race when their world allows them to remain comfortably, oblivious, and racially ignorant? After all, we live in a society that customarily names the victims of racist systems without naming the oppressor or those who yield the power.

The lack of racial stamina didn't just rest with these two women. My white supervisors who testified to being afraid of me were visibly defensive on the witness stand because they were being included in an uncomfortable conversation about race-based advantages. I soon learned that it was the discomfort of the topic itself that would turn several of my former white coworker "friends" into silent enemies. I went from being the only black person at their homes for barbecues, housewarmings, and baby showers to not even being worthy of a return text message.

My hurt feelings and confusion started me on a quest for knowledge in hopes of interrupting and dismantling racial ignorance through conversations. I've learned that the social norms, policies, and procedures moving us into preexisting racial frameworks are always in motion. And without a deliberate, committed resistance to systemic and institutionalized racism, nothing will change. But how can anyone resist or fight against a truth that the privileged class is not willing to talk about or acknowledge?

CHAPTER 1

In the Beginning

I normally claim St. Louis, Missouri, as my home. But really, I'm a small-town girl who has always been mesmerized by the shimmer of city lights and intimidated by the city streets. I grew up in Moberly, Missouri, a town of less than fourteen thousand people. But I loved the drives to St. Louis with my family to see relatives who lived in what I considered, at the time, a big exciting city.

In 1982, as a six-year-old girl living in Moberly, I remember my uncle Burlington Benson's picture flashing on the ten o'clock news. At the time, I didn't know anything was wrong, but the news anchor quickly informed me he'd been missing from his St. Louis home, and his body had been located in East St. Louis. Immediately, I could see the pain in my father's eyes seeing his baby brother's picture on the evening news. His eyes filled with tears that slowly streamed down his face. I learned that day that television news was bad, and I decided that I would never watch it again. A commitment I maintained throughout my adolescent and preteen years. I did not watch the news.

When I was twelve years old, because of the realities of my father's alcoholism, chronic unemployment and the subsequent financial toll, my mother decided to move back home to St. Louis for better work opportunities and to be closer to her family. We temporarily moved into my uncle Robert Robinson's three-story home with my extended family. It was a huge transition. We moved from a small town, dominated by white people in Moberly, to the city of St. Louis. My personal commitment to not watching the news held strong, but now, being in my uncle's home, the evening news monopolized television screens in what was now a shared family room. The murders and gun violence still permeated the newscasts and deepened my resolve to either walk out of the room or close my eyes. Until one day, my uncle Robert, a stout dark-skinned man of average height and great financial means in my young mind because he owned and drove his own taxicab, told me while watching the news that I looked like Robin Smith. Robin Smith, a beautiful brown-skinned black woman, was the main anchor at the CBS affiliate in St. Louis. Growing up at a time when I didn't see a lot of black women on television, I was so flattered that my uncle looked at me and thought I resembled a woman of such beauty and poise.

From that day, I didn't watch the news for the information, but I wanted to see if I could see myself in the impeccably dressed Robin Smith's flawless delivery of the tragic news of the day.

Several months after, my mom secured a factory job and found a two-family flat to move her husband and three children into on the northside of St. Louis. After a number of fights while attending school in the St. Louis City Public School system, one in which I got punched in the face by a boy while walking home from school. My older sister got her head busted trying to protect me. My mother enrolled my sister and I in St. Louis' desegregation program. A program designed to help integrate public schools. We continued living in St. Louis city, but each morning, my middle sister and I spent nearly two hours on a yellow school bus heading to south county as students of the Lindbergh School District.

As an eighth grader, I was back in my comfort zone. I was once again one of maybe three black students in the classroom. I spent each day feeling like I didn't quite belong but thinking this was a good school and a safe place to learn. By ninth grade, I was excited to join my sister at the high school. During my freshman year, I was enrolled in a couple of International Baccalaureate advanced courses, so I went from being one of three black students in the classroom to many times the only one.

During my initial tour of the high school campus, I was immediately drawn to the print room of the school newspaper. It was big, busy, and had a lot of paper scraps on the floor. I knew I wanted to be a part of whatever happened in this room. I joined the *Pilot* school newspaper staff. I was the only black student on the newspaper staff, and that didn't bother me one bit.

My involvement in my school newspaper opened the door to my first flight in November of 1993. The journalism teacher took the entire newspaper staff to a journalism conference in Washington, DC. I'll never forget being amazed when I looked out the airplane window and saw that we were flying above the clouds. I truly felt like I was closer to God. This experience, coupled with our exploration of Washington, DC, birthed my love for travel.

I went to a few journalism trainings throughout my high school career, including some through the Greater St. Louis Association of Black Journalists and a prestigious journalism workshop for minority students at the University of Missouri-Columbia. Through these experiences, I received a true glimpse of the power of the media. I could see clearly how the local news helped shape and challenge the minds of viewers. I wanted to harness the power of the media to challenge how people saw the world. Through these trainings, I explored my love of writing but realized that I thrived from the immediate gratification of television newscasts. I loved the nowness, the urgency, the energy of doing something new and different every day. By the time I graduated from Lindbergh High School, I knew that I wanted to be a television news reporter.

During my junior year, my best friend, Mandisa, and her mother invited me along for a drive to Atlanta, Georgia, to see her brother at Morehouse College. I was utterly amazed at seeing so many black students at the Atlanta University Center, proudly pursuing higher education. I distinctly recall seeing a student driving a fancy red sports car on James P. Brawley Drive on the Clark Atlanta University campus. I was in awe of the intelligence and wealth these black people possessed and proudly represented on these campuses. After hanging out at Morehouse College and Clark Atlanta University, I knew that I wanted to attend a historically black college or university, also known as an HBCU. Initially, I enrolled in Dillard University in New Orleans, Louisiana. After a year, I transferred to Clark Atlanta University to take advantage the university's television station and the fact that the city was hosting the 1996 Olympic Games. That experience helped me land a research reporter position at CNN in the fall of 1997. The position was unpaid, which was typical in 1997, but it was highly competitive among budding journalists throughout the country. I distinctly remember working with broadcast journalism students from both Harvard University and the University of Missouri-Columbia. The Harvard student's parents paid for an apartment in Downtown Atlanta so their daughter could take advantage of this opportunity. I remember feeling so proud of myself for transferring to CAU because I knew, otherwise, there was no way I would have had the opportunity to intern at CNN. At the time, both of my parents were battling different forms of cancer; neither of them had an income.

Attending Clark Atlanta University became a great, much-needed equalizer for me when it came to black people. My childhood upbringing and media programming taught me that "white" schools, neighborhoods, and people were good. Attending Clark Atlanta University and living in the south taught me that I had a lot more to learn about people of color. People who looked just like me.

First Job

I graduated from Clark Atlanta University in July of 1998 with a bachelor's degree in mass media arts with an emphasis in radio/television/film. In September of the same year, my mother died of cancer while my father was batting esophageal cancer. In November of 1998, I was offered my first one-man band reporter position at a television station in St. Joseph, Missouri. Its designated market area (DMA) ranking was 198 at the time. There were only 212 DMAs in the nation, which are ranked-based on the population of the city. St. Joseph is a small town, very low on the ranking, which matched the starting salary. It was low. The one-man band reporter position meant I would have to set up, shoot, edit, write, and front my own stories every day. The job I accepted paid $13,500 dollars a year. I was over the moon to be starting my career as a television news reporter in Missouri.

Despite my excitement, the reality of being on my own and making so little money was tough. Now that my mother had passed, I had no financial safety net. My father also lost his battle with esophageal cancer within two years of me starting the job, so not only was I working while always broke, but now I was an orphan.

I spent about two and a half years working at KQTV in St. Joseph. During that time, I was promoted to weekend anchor, where I worked beside a white male coworker every weekend. An anchor position I truly enjoyed. Despite identifying as a reporter, I started coveting the weekend anchor position during my latter years at Clark Atlanta University. The weekend anchor at WSB-TV in Atlanta at that time was Shaunya Chavis. Chavis visited one of my classes at CAU to talk about her daily job duties and her passion for the business. She was so kind, poised, professional, and beautifully black. I'll never forget the classy drop-top BMW Chavis drove off campus. At that moment, I knew I wanted to follow in her footsteps. I wanted to represent to other people what Chavis represented to me: beauty, power, authority, and an undeniable voice that could challenge the minds of masses.

When it was time for me to leave St. Joseph, I knew I wanted to move as an anchor and stay within driving distance of my family in St. Louis. I was offered my next job over the phone after sending in my résumé tape, followed by another tape of my most recent work. The news director hired me as an anchor/reporter but did not confirm which show I would be working on. She was considering me for the 5:00 o'clock evening anchor position and the weekend evening anchor position. I was so excited about getting my next job and make a whopping $28,000 a year that I didn't care which show I anchored. My sisters drove to St. Joseph, packed my one-bedroom apartment onto a U-Haul, and we were on our way to Decatur, Illinois, so I could anchor and report at WAND-TV.

I quickly found a one-bedroom apartment in Decatur, not far from the station. Much like St. Joseph, Decatur was a small midwest town with few people of color. However, because of my small town background, assimilating and adapting were second nature. I was ready to share my craft with the people of Central Illinois.

On my first day on the job, I was looking forward to meeting the black female news director who hired me. Unfortunately, after I arrived, the executive producer told me that she had left the station, and he was in charge. Within a few weeks, the executive producer assigned me to the weekend anchor position and promoted a current white female employee into the five o'clock anchor position. I was disappointed that I was not in the five o'clock anchor position, but I was grateful to be doing what I loved, just two hours from home.

I coanchored the weekend newscasts with my white male coworker and quickly met the movers and shakers in Decatur. Just two hours from home, my more than two years in Decatur went by quickly. This position, much like the previous one, required that I worked every weekend. As a single woman with no children, I didn't mind the sacrifice. After all, I wasn't shooting all my stories anymore, which was great.

Kansas City or Bust

During my time in St. Joseph, my coworkers and I would drive to Kansas City to shop at Metro North Mall, go clubbing, or just walk around and window-shop at the posh Country Club Plaza. Being members of the media, we would get media passes to cover the Kansas City Chiefs football team and take full advantage of the free food and fun that accompanied covering the team. Through these experiences, which included attending my first NFL game, I fell in love with Kansas City. In fact, I met one of my dearest friends in Kansas City, Tiffany Dwight Estell. She actually came to KQTV in St. Joseph to audition for my weekend coanchor position in 2000. The minute Tiffany (a black woman) and I met, we knew there was no way that they were going to allow two black women to anchor the weekend newscasts together. Nonetheless, we quickly became good friends. It was quite common for me to spend my off days in Kansas City shopping with Tiffany or drive to Kansas City after work on a Saturday night to go to a club and hang out with other friends. Kansas City quickly started feeling like my second home. It felt like a small town, but in my mind, it possessed all the fun and excitement of a big city.

As my third year at WAND-TV approached, I knew it was time to go after Kansas City. I sent tapes to stations with open positions and drove the five hours from Decatur to Kansas City to meet news directors, spending my own money. At one point, my friend Tiffany had a reporter friend at the NBC affiliate in Kansas City who put in her notice that she was resigning. That friend was a black female reporter/ anchor. Tiffany notified me. She and I knew this could be my opportunity. They were losing a black woman, so they would be more receptive to hiring a black woman. So I looked up the news director's name and made a cold call. I had to sell myself on the phone in hopes of creating my own interview opportunity.

These cold calls would start with an introduction of myself and my work, followed by "I'll be in Kansas City next week. I would love to meet you and get some feedback on my work." If they agreed to meet with me, I would make plans to stay with friends and gas up my car for my "go-see." This method proved successful in getting me my very first job in St. Joseph, so I tried it again in Kansas City. A lot of news directors would gladly take advantage of this free interview opportunity, seeing as they didn't have to pay for flights, gas, or food.

After one go-see, an interview, and another follow-up meeting to interview with the general manager, I was hired at KSHB-TV in Kansas City, Missouri, in March of 2004. I accepted the general assignment reporter position because I was headed to my dream city, and after talking to the news director about my professional goals, I had no doubt that I would climb the newsroom ladder like I had in my previous positions.

Kansas City, here I come!

CHAPTER 2

Kansas City, Here I Come!

After a brief apartment search, I settled into a one-bedroom apartment in Mission, Kansas. It was a quick twelve-minute drive to the station, and I was stoked! I was assigned to the morning show reporter position. So I had to be at work at three thirty in the morning, five days a week. It was a huge adjustment as far as sleeping. I bought black light blocking curtains and tried to put myself on a strict sleep schedule. The black curtains worked; my strict sleep schedule did not.

The morning show gave me the opportunity to fully develop as a live late-breaking news reporter. As a reporter, I did several live shots throughout the morning and live interviews on breaking news scenes. As the news director at the time said, it was a great training ground for reporters moving into larger markets.

Both St. Joseph and Decatur were smaller markets with limited live capabilities. This station in Kansas City had plenty of live trucks to choose from each morning.

I had no problem waking up at two o'clock in the morning to get dressed and ready for work, but my social life did. My dating life did not fit into my strict sleep schedule…at all!

Something as simple as a happy hour was a no-no and would violate my sleep schedule. I usually missed my goal of getting eight hours of sleep each night because of my 6:00 p.m. bedtime. But seriously, what single twenty-seven-year-old woman wants to go to bed at 6:00 p.m.? But I definitely felt the repercussions of my bad decisions the next day. After several months on the job, my decisions and days were motivated exclusively by what would get me to sleep faster. I was constantly planning my days around the probability of me getting more sleep.

After the morning show live shots, I was paired with a photographer to work on stories for later newscasts. I distinctly remember working with a white male photographer on a story and him becoming frustrated with me. In his frustration, he yelled and cursed at me with a battery of expletives, including "what the fuck." As a young reporter, I was humiliated, angered, and intimidated by his choice of words. I reported the exchange to my white female morning executive producer. Her response was, "He's just like that. You just have to stand up to him."

It didn't take long for that photographer's rage to take aim again. This time, I was committed to "putting him in his place," but I could not find the words or the nerve to confront this stout older white male who for whatever reason had no plans or obligation to respect me.

Again, when he cursed at me, I said nothing. But this time, when I returned to the station, I bypassed my executive producer and reported his conduct to the woman in human resources at KSHB-TV. I explained to her that growing up, I heard curse words. I even heard my father use such foul language, but my father would have never directed such vile language toward me. I explained to her that me allowing this man to talk to me in this way felt disrespectful to not only to me but to my now-deceased father.

I don't know what the HR woman did with my complaint. I was never called into an investigation or told of any disciplinary action. However, it would be years before I would work one-on-one with that photographer again.

Despite being a morning show reporter, I would get opportunities to fill in on the anchor desk and on the dayside shift. Dayside shifts were from 9:30 a.m. until 6:30 p.m., which for television newspeople is the closest you'll probably get to a normal schedule. Thankfully, my news director saw the energy and contributions that I brought to the dayside shift that were not consistently present on the morning show, in part because I was always tired. She told me she was moving me to a weekend dayside reporter shift. I didn't want to give up my weekends off, but I was elated to stop reporting to work at three thirty in the morning.

Moved to Dayside Reporter

The move to dayside was an exciting change. I had to adjust to a new batch of people, but now I had the opportunity to bring my interests and story ideas to the table as a dayside reporter. I was also included in the fill-in anchor rotation, which was something the news director assured me of when I was hired.

At the time, I was the only black reporter on the team, and we had one black anchor. A dynamic that I was familiar with, thanks to my time in Decatur, Illinois, and St. Joseph, Missouri.

In 2005, the station created a midday show called *Kansas City Live*. When we were told about the new Monday through Friday lifestyle magazine show, they had already selected a white woman who would anchor the show. I was surprised and disappointed that there were no job postings or auditions for the position. Nonetheless, I was still encouraged that the show would present more opportunities for me to fill in and prove myself as an anchor.

In a matter of time, I was moved from the weekend dayside reporter to the nightside Monday through Friday reporter. This meant working until eleven o'clock at night, but now I had weekends off, which I looked forward to.

While working the nightside shift, it became clear to me that the nightside work schedule sucked when it came to dating. Again, as a single black woman, it meant no happy hours throughout the week, and if I wanted to hangout after work, I'd essentially be meeting someone at midnight. And we all know…Christian singles have no business "dating" at those hours.

After more than a year on the nightside shift, I informed my news director that I wanted off nightside and would prefer to go dayside. She told me that she considered me one of her strongest reporters and would keep me nightside.

Disappointed and frustrated, I considered moving back to St. Louis if the right employment opportunity arose. I submitted a tape to the CBS affiliate. The news director showed interest and invited me in for an interview. For some unknown reason, I volunteered to drive in for the interview even though the station offered to fly me in. I'll never understand why I felt compelled to save this multimillion-dollar media conglomerate money. Crazy.

The interview, in my opinion, went well. I even got the opportunity to meet Robin Smith, the anchor I grew up watching, hoping to somehow see myself in the beauty and poise she displayed each day on the news. She was as poised, welcoming, and beautiful as I had remembered from my childhood.

Despite my e-mails and casual "checking in" calls, the news director in St. Louis repeatedly told me they had not made a decision, and I was still being considered. I was being extremely persistent because, at this point in my life, I was no longer dating. I was engaged to my now husband, and we were deciding where we were going to plant our roots. Are we staying in Kansas City, his hometown and a city that I had grown to love, or are we making a move to St. Louis to be closer to my family, which would be a new adventure for him?

Almost a month after my interview, the news director in St. Louis informed me that she went with another candidate. In hindsight, I believe sharing my disdain for nightside reporting affected her decision, but nonetheless, it gave necessary closure to help my fiancé and I make a decision about our future. As a self-employed contractor, who invested in real estate, he was ready to make a final decision about our future.

At my station, I had moved into a freelance reporter position because I did not want to sign another contract and be banished to nightside reporting. During this time, my news director announced that she accepted a job as a general manager at another station. Within weeks, another news director was hired. Shortly after his arrival, he saw my work, offered me a contract with a pay increase, and told me I did not have to work nightside.

He would not allow me to go to the coveted Monday through Friday dayside position. Instead, he put me back to the weekend shift. A shift I gladly accepted because then I could continue doing the job I loved in a city that I adopted as my own and marry my fiancé and best friend.

The new news director, a short middle-aged white male, was direct but very casual. At times, he would make what seemed to be inappropriate comments about some reporters; but followed by his smile and laugh, they didn't seem to bother anyone.

He decided to cancel the midday show and start a weekend morning newscast. In my mind, this weekend morning newscast was my opportunity to get back on the anchor desk. I was already working weekends, so the viewers knew me. I had already worked the morning show, so I knew I could adjust to the early morning hours, and I was a primary fill-in on the anchor desk. I just knew I had this. To further tip the scales in my favor, I collaborated with a white male reporter who had recently been hired. I thought if we presented ourselves as a package deal, a black woman and a white male, this would have been a sure bet. I interviewed for the job, read a few shows, and the news director said I was a finalist for the position.

I was disappointed when my news director announced the new morning anchor team. They chose the white male reporter I auditioned with and a white female Monday through Friday reporter. I would later learn that she didn't even apply for the job because she enjoyed weekends off with her husband. The news director insisted on her taking the position. The white reporter who got the job was a beautiful, thin blonde-haired white woman. I could not help but wonder, "If I looked like her, would I have been good enough? How does someone get a position that they didn't even apply for?"

Nonetheless, I still believed that one day, I would get the opportunity to anchor my own show at the station. I just had to be patient and continue proving my value as both an anchor and a reporter at the station.

Despite not getting the promotion, I enjoyed having more people of color in the newsroom. The station had hired another black female reporter and a black male reporter.

The election of Barack Obama and the 2009 inauguration was huge for the journalists of color in the newsroom. At this point, I was one of three African American reporters who was excited about the historic event. I proposed covering the event live in Washington, DC. Initially, the news director hesitated but soon agreed that viewers would benefit from live local coverage of the first African American man being sworn into office. He agreed that the event needed local coverage but told me that the station did not have enough money in its budget to pay for flights or to pay overtime for the assignment. I did not skip a beat in telling him that I would be willing to drive to Washington, DC, from Kansas City, Missouri, and work for straight pay so I could cover the inauguration. No overtime to further prove my drive and dedication to E. W. Scripps.

He smiled and accepted my compromise. My photographer and I immediately started making plans to drive the sixteen-hour drive to Washington, DC. Due to budget issues. We had to book a hotel in Flintstone, Maryland, and use public transportation to get to the US Capitol and the National Mall in Washington, DC.

The trip was both exhilarating and exhausting from being in the nation's capital on this historic day to navigating the DC metro on foot with tons of equipment. It was a lot.

Upon our return to Kansas City, I turned in my time card as did my photographer. Within days, I received a call from the human resources department. The HR manager questioned why my time card did not have any overtime hours but the photographer's did. I explained to her that the news director told me that the station could not afford overtime for the trip. She explained to me that the photographer got paid overtime, and I should be paid as well. She told me that she would alter my time card to match the hours the photographer worked. She also promised to follow up with the news director about the pay discrepancy.

At the time, I was more worried about my white male news director being mad at me for now having to pay me for my work. Now, I clearly see that he would expect a black woman to be willing to work for free, but he would not have expected or even asked that of the male photographer.

In 2009, the same news director managed another employee shake-up. The white male weekend anchor resigned. This change left the weekend morning anchor desk open. I applied again.

During the candidate search and interview process, the news director got fired. Rumors surrounding his swift departure included a sexual relationship with a white female producer and the firing of a reporter to promote the producer who doubled as his sex kitten.

Shortly after the now new white female news director arrived, her first order of business was to fill the weekend morning anchor position. I went through the meet and greet and interview process with the new boss. She was a stout redheaded white woman with an abrasive personality. During the interview for the position, she seemed genuinely pleased with my anchoring. She told me that she did open the position up to outside candidates but assured me that I was among the top three finalists for the position. Again, I felt good about the exchange. I was still a primary fill-in anchor for the weekend shows, and I knew they valued me as an employee, so why wouldn't they give me an opportunity to grow with the station?

"We just need some fresh meat," that's what the white female news director said to me as she explained why I would not be the station's new weekend morning anchor. I was again disappointed... but not crushed. She assured me that I did a great job as an anchor and would still be allowed to fill in, but they just needed new faces in the newsroom.

In a matter of days, the station-wide e-mail went out announcing who the new weekend morning anchor would be. The new hire was a biracial woman who grew up in the Kansas City metro area and used to be a Kansas City Chiefs' cheerleader. The women at the station immediately starting googling her name. One found a picture of her in a green pageant costume and said she looked like the main character from the Avatar movie.

I chuckled at the comment but knew that was insecurity talking on my colleague's part. This woman was absolutely beautiful. She had a thin frame, flawless skin with an ethnically ambiguous tone, and long dark hair. Somehow the color in her skin and her undeniable beauty made my defeat easier to accept. I didn't get the promotion, but at least it went to a woman of color.

CHAPTER 3

Opportunities for Growth?

My mission to grow at KSHB-TV continued over the years. I applied for more opportunities to move into weekend anchor positions as I continued to excel as a reporter. In 2011, I covered a story about a man whose mother died when he was in prison. When he got out of prison, he learned that his mother had been cremated, and no one ever picked up her ashes from the funeral home. He reached out to me because he was impressed by my work, and he learned that the funeral home that performed the cremation had closed. After doing the story with him and contacting the owner of the property, we were able to locate the ashes of his deceased mother in the basement of the now boarded-up funeral home. We also discovered hundreds of other black boxes full of ashes on the shelves of this abandoned funeral home. When I turned my story in that day and reported my findings to my news director and the special projects producer, they immediately congratulated me on my findings and for following through with such an interesting story.

Within days, the special projects executive producer told me that they were turning my story over to the investigative reporter. When I questioned the decision, they told me I would not have time to do the research needed to find the family members of the other ashes that were left behind. At the time, I was excited to see how excited they were about the stories I had already done. Stories that I had shot, wrote, and edited on my own. It took a while for me to realize that they were looking for an opportunity to showcase the white male reporter who had already surpassed my salary despite being lower in seniority and experience.

The white reporter did a number of follow-up stories, and the station submitted our work to the Mid-America Emmy Awards for the National Academy of Television Arts and Sciences. That was the first time that any of my work had been submitted for the annual award. Sure enough, my story lead to me and the station's lead investigative reporter winning our first Emmy. The station would go on to submit and pay for more entries on his behalf in subsequent years. They never submitted any more stories on my behalf. But nonetheless, I was now an Emmy Award-winning journalist.

In my efforts to be positioned for more anchor opportunities, I agreed to work four ten-hour days each week in 2011. At that time, it put me back on weekends, but I was willing to take a less desirable shift because the news director said it would better position me to fill in on the anchor desk. The young white reporter who worked the same schedule prior to me was promoted to a morning anchor position at an E.W. Scripps station in Indianapolis. So again, I thought, if I just stayed patient and kept my nose to the grind, I too would get an opportunity to grow into an anchor position.

In February 2013, I gave birth to my first son. At this point, I had been married five years, and my husband had grown tired of playing the maybe-next-year game when it came to having kids. I've always wanted children, but I wanted to be further up on the food chain and pay scale before starting a family. I never wanted to be the pregnant general assignment reporter at the crime scene. But I was.

Nonetheless, my son gave me a new vision and a new purpose. I was so happy to now have my new definition. My top priority of the day was not finding relevant stories to pitch or hitting a flawless live shot. Now my top priority, the thing that kept me up at night, was creating a safe, loving home for my son.

In 2012, the station fired my news director and hired a new general manager. I certainly did not want to meet my new GM while pregnant, but what choice did I have? During my maternity leave, the new news director started. I reached out to her on the phone, welcomed her to the station, and told her I was interested in growing into an anchor position.

The news director who was fired was a white female, and the new news director was also a white woman. For some reason, I was surprised that the new GM didn't hire a man. But nonetheless, I was looking forward to meeting my new boss and proving myself yet again.

In May of 2013, I headed back to the newsroom ready to prove to yet another news director that I am qualified for the job and worthy of growing with the company. Shortly before my return, I learned that the contract of the beautiful biracial woman who was hired for the weekend morning show was not renewed. A white female reporter, Lindsay Shively, had been promoted into her position. I had expressed to both the GM and the new news director my desire to grow into an anchor position, but clearly, no one considered me for the position when it was open.

Over the next two years, there were a number of changes that lead to openings at the weekend anchor desk, but none that lead to my promotion. In 2014, I applied to be a leadership champion at the station. This unpaid position allows employees to go through corporate sponsored leadership training to help make the newsroom a better, more productive environment. I didn't get that position either. It went to a white man and woman at KSHB-TV. Nonetheless, every two to three years, I'd be offered a new contract but never a promotion.

Finally, one day, it dawned on me. They don't want to see me as an anchor, and they never will. That reality hurt, but I still felt committed to the station, knowing that I'm valued as a good reporter. The investigative reporter left in 2015, and I decided to go for the full-time investigative reporter position. At the time, I thought it was a no-brainer. I am a good reporter, I have more than twelve years of experience with the company, and I earned my NATAS Emmy for "Continuing Coverage." This promotion would allow me to focus on impactful stories that matter, have weekends off, and I'd move up the pay scale, which was always part of the goal.

I put in a formal application and interviewed with the news director. During the interview, I told the news director I would work as the "fill-in" investigator as she interviewed for the position just to prove my worth.

I tried to further sell her on my skills and ability by telling her I would guarantee a story four days a week as an investigator. I knew that generating enough stories was a problem for previous investigators. So I was promising a lot for investigative pieces, but I knew I could make it happen if given the opportunity to prove myself.

She declined my offer and kindly told me that they wanted someone with previous "data mining" experience in an investigative unit for the position. Her simple, matter-of-fact conversation quickly convinced me that I, a reporter with more than a decade of experience, was not qualified for the promotion.

In April 2015, the station sent out an e-mail announcing they had found the next investigative reporter. The younger white female had worked as a weekend anchor/reporter for less than three years. She had nine years of nursing experience. She too had no "data mining" experience in an investigative unit, but nonetheless, she was hired at KSHB-TV as an investigator. Why her? Why not me?

Tension Builds

It's clear that I'm not seen as an anchor. It's clear that I'm not seen as an investigative reporter, but can I at least get off weekends now? I agreed to go back to weekends to better position myself to fill-in anchor in 2011. Now with staff and shift changes, I asked to move back to a Monday through Friday shift, which would allow me to spend more time with my husband and son.

The news director agreed to talk to me about my request, and to my shock and humiliation, she told me that I was an inconsistent, unbalanced reporter with performance issues. During this April of 2015 conversation, she went on to say that I wasn't a strong enough reporter to work a Monday through Friday dayside shift. When I reminded her of my 2014 review that was completed just a few months prior, she told me she was "sorry" and that I had not received an adequate review of my work. In that review, my immediate supervisor documented that I was "fully meeting the expectations of my position" in all categories. A review that my news director had signed off on. I lost it. I literally broke down in tears and ran out of her office. I could not believe that my more than twelve years of reporting, my Emmy, and the multiple contracts offered to me by the station didn't even earn me weekends off.

I sat in my car and called one of my closest friends, Chelsea Clark. She coached me into drying my tears and going back to work. I sent an e-mail from my car to memorialize the moment and inform them that I would be back to work momentarily. It was at that moment that I realized that my day was not coming; my number would never be called. I, as a black woman, would not have any opportunities to grow with this news organization. I would always be seen as the support staff to help others achieve greatness. I knew then that I had to fight.

─────∿∿◦◖⟳◦⟲⟩◦◖⟲◦∿∿─────

CHAPTER 4

EEOC Complaint/Lawsuit Filed

My first tactical maneuver to challenge E. W. Scripps and KSHB-TV took me to human resources. The white HR woman listened to my complaints about differential treatment, being overlooked, and the offense I took in being told that I'm not even good enough to get off weekends. The agreed-upon resolution between human resources and management was to create more feedback opportunities for me. I knew this was just another diversion, but I was ready to showcase and defend my work.

The next move was to report my experience to corporate HR. During my list of grievances during our telephone conversation, the woman did not offer an intervention at KSHB-TV; instead, she informed me that the company would support me in moving on and finding a new job. I was shocked by her response. She basically told me that nothing would be changing, and that my best option was to leave. This was devastating to me because I had a two-year-old that I was responsible for, and my husband and I were actively trying for number two. How could I go to my husband yet again and say now is not a good time to grow our family because I think my bosses are trying to force me out?

On May 20, 2015, I filed a formal charge of discrimination against KSHB-TV. It read that the cause of discrimination was a continuing action of race discrimination, retaliation, and a hostile work environment.

The very same week, I was sent to Mosby, Missouri, to cover weekend flooding following the governor's visit. Despite flooded roadways and weak signals, I did a short video followed by sound-bites stories for every newscast. After my five o'clock live shot, my dayside executive producer called and told us to put file video of the weekend flooding into the story. I told my photographer what she wanted, he added the video. We proceeded to hit live shots for every show.

The next day, the dayside EP and I met for a feedback session. During the session, she complimented my social media presence, story characters, and asked why I didn't use file video in my five o'clock story. I explained to her that as an on-the-ground reporter, I wanted to move the story forward. I explained to her that we had people who lost their homes, a flooded-out police department, and fresh sound from the governor, saying financial help may not be coming. I told her that the inverted pyramid of storytelling says start big and go small, so I would expect the anchor toss to show the old video, and I would bring viewers a fresh new look.

She clapped back, saying as a veteran reporter, I should have known to use the file video. I responded saying, as a veteran reporter, I know my job is to report on what's happening now, not what happened two days ago. She accused me of not listening, got up from her chair, and left.

I returned to my desk, which was in the same row, and continued working to the end of my shift.

I decided to call the station's EthicsPoint number. I was surprised by the EP's reaction to a mere conversation about the use of file video, and at this point, I was always in defense mode. I called the 1-800 number and filed a verbal complaint to memorialize my experience.

The human resources lady called me on May 21, 2015, and asked if I could come to the station. I told her my schedule would not allow it, so we agreed to meet on May 26, 2015 because it was a holiday weekend. I just happened to be scheduled to fill in on the anchor day that weekend, so I anchored the newscasts over the weekend and reported to the HR office the following Tuesday.

When I walked into the office, my news director and the HR lady were present. The HR lady informed me that I was being suspended without pay for my conversation with the dayside EP. I asked what I had done wrong. She said the conversation was inappropriate. I said, "What did I say that was inappropriate?" and asked why I wasn't involved in the investigation. She said they talked to everyone they needed to talk to. I again asked, "What did I say that was inappropriate?" She told me that it was not what I said but how I said it. I then questioned why I was being suspended seeing as I had nothing in my personnel file. She said my "tone was so egregious in nature that it warranted an immediate suspension."

I got up, gathered my things, and left the building to serve my two-day suspension. By this time, I had already consulted an attorney. I called the law firm to inform them of my suspension.

After serving my suspension, I returned to work, knowing that I would have to document and challenge everything, or my job would be gone. I found out in late May that I was pregnant with my second child, which furthered my resolve to protect my integrity as a professional journalist and my job as a mother of what will soon be two children.

Despite my warrior spirit, it gets hard preparing for battle every day. There is no room for creativity, second opinions, or genuine interests. I'm now here to get my job done and be prepared if someone challenged my work. This is a stressful way to live, but I had to create an impermeable barrier that they could not penetrate... because it would cost me my income and my children, their insurance if I made a mistake.

Despite my armor, my fear of losing my job while pregnant overtook me. I started looking for part-time jobs that could grow into full-time work if I got fired. I applied for a job with American Airlines as a part-time customer service agent. I managed to get through training, but working both jobs became impossible as a now thirty-nine-year-old pregnant woman. I had to let the airline job go and focus on keeping my job despite the isolation, nit-picking, glaring stares, and the need to prove and reprove my story pitch of the day is worthy day after day. This was horrible. I felt anxious, fearful, and powerless every day.

I was honest with my obstetrician about the stress of the job. She suggested that I take an antidepressant to help me deal with my bouts of tears and frustrations that I would often live out in the privacy of a bathroom stall. She wrote me a prescription for an antidepressant. Full of shame for being so weak, I filled the prescription. That night, despite my doctor telling me it would not hurt my unborn child, I lay in bed worried to death about the side effects. What if this medicine hurts my baby? The next day, Friday, July 24, 2015, I contacted the E. W. Scripps Leave Administration. I requested and took a ninety-day FMLA leave. This unpaid time off gave me job and benefits protection as I got through the first trimester of my pregnancy. My husband and I had to adjust to the financial toll of living without my income, but mentally, I needed a break from the psychological war zone that was now my place of work.

FMLA Leave of Absence

I had just signed another one-year contract before taking the leave, which helped me to fully unplug from work and focus on my personal and professional fight to hold my employer accountable. I needed the leave to clear my head and to map out a plan. This also allowed me to experience life as a "kept woman." As someone who's worked since I was fourteen years old, I had become accustomed to working and taking care of myself. Now I got to test-drive truly living by my faith in God and under my husband's headship. Living without an income and truly enjoying my time with my family gave me a glimpse of what life without TV news could be like. And surprisingly, I didn't hate it. I felt fully present and defined by being a wife and mother.

During my leave, I got a few calls from a photographer friend, but for the most part, my coworkers had no idea what I was doing or when I was coming back, and I was okay with that.

When I returned to work, very few people asked me where I had been. In fact, many went back to only talking to me when the news director and the assistant news director were not in the newsroom. Nonetheless, I felt fully charged for the fight to prove that KSHB-TV discriminates against people of color. I had filed my complaint with the EEOC, but I was still waiting to receive my right to sue from the Missouri Human Rights Commission. My initial complaint was amended, which further delayed the results of the investigation.

But finally, in September of 2016, the Missouri Commission on Human Rights issued a notice of "your right to sue" in my case, which basically meant my attorney had the right to move forward and file a lawsuit.

I knew that the station's attorney had, according to court documents, "unequivocally" denied that it had discriminated or retaliated against me in any manner. They said my "generic" allegations of race discrimination and retaliation were factually and legally without merit. The station had even asked the Missouri Commission on Human Rights to dismiss my complaint in its entirety. So you can only imagine how relieved and elated I was to hear that the investigator who took all of our statements agreed that my case did, in fact, have merit and deserved to be heard by a judge and quite possibly a jury of my peers.

My attorney had ninety days to file his lawsuit, and they moved quickly.

The pettiness at work also continued in hopes of forcing me out or giving themselves grounds to fire me. In August, I asked my news director if I could come in at nine o'clock in the morning instead of eighty thirty so I could drop my now pre-K son off at school. I agreed to shave the thirty minutes from my lunch break. She called me into her office and essentially told me no. She went on to tell me that my personal life should not affect my workday. I made other arrangements for my three-year-old son to be dropped off at school.

Around the same time, a photographer was called away to breaking news while editing our package. I was asked to quickly finish the edit and send it in. After the story aired, it was brought to the station's attention that a man in the video the photographer shot had a curse word on his shirt. The photographer shot the video and edited the video into the story. But because I finished the story and didn't catch his mistake before I sent it in, I was written up for the video making it on television; the photographer was not. That happened in September of 2016. The same month I was granted the right to sue.

CHAPTER 5

Retaliation Continues

The nit-picking of my work without detailed examples and bogus write-ups continued. Another photographer mistakenly put a picture of a website, also known as a screengrab, that contained curse words into a story in August of 2017.

Again, I was now responsible for this professional photographer's work. In this situation, I wasn't even in the truck when the package was being edited and sent. In fact, another photographer was sent to the live shot location to help this photographer because of his limited live truck experience. Nonetheless, I was the only person suspended for three days for the error. In this case, the black male photographer jumped to my defense, explaining that I had nothing to do with the screengrab making it on air. His words held no power.

These suspensions and reprimands just solidified my conviction that they were just trying to find a reason or create a paper trail so they could fire me. I knew they wanted me out of the newsroom. This was embarrassing for me as a professional journalist, who had never been expected to supervise professional photographers before, but I knew this had nothing to do with their unfortunate mistakes and everything to do with the station trying to get rid of me because I dared to file a complaint and a lawsuit against the company.

Fired/Lawsuit Amended

The jury trial in my discrimination case was supposed to begin in April of 2018. The judge had only slated a week for the trial. Both sides agreed that they needed two weeks. The trial was continued to August of 2018. A new trial date that was further delayed by Facebook posts and my termination.

May 10, 2018, was a normal reporting day for me at KSHB-TV. I pitched my stories, set up the interviews, and hit my live shots like any other day. That night, I attended a self-care workshop at the Uzazi Village on Troost Avenue. The presentation given by a woman of color included a written questionnaire and assessment about stress. I scored 97 points out of 100 on the stress test. I was surprised at how stressed out I was, but I knew that the burden of this lawsuit and this job was showing up in my body, mentally and physically. Leaving the presentation, I decided to take a mental health day the next day, which was May 11. I would focus on my son, who'd been dealing with ear problems, and take some time for self-care. On my way home, I called my job and let them know that I had to take care of some personal obligations and would not be at work the following Friday morning.

The next morning started fine. My son said his ear was better, so I let him go to school, and I settled into the self-care plans the presenter outlined the night before.

Sometime before 11:00 a.m., I got a phone call from the news station. I checked the message, and it was a call from the human resources manager. Seeing as I had called off, I called him back immediately and left a message. Within minutes, he called me back again and informed me that I was being suspended with pay for creating a hostile work environment based on race and sex. I immediately started asking questions out of my utter confusion. He refused to answer any questions. He simply restated that I was being suspended for creating a hostile work environment based on race and sex. He said they had received complaints from two people at work and told me that I would be suspended as the complaints were investigated.

Despite my confusion and offense, I accepted my punishment as the call ended. For the next week, I played in my head who I could have offended and how. Seeing as the complaint was based on race and sex, I was focused on white men. What had I done or said to the white men who worked with me in the newsroom or in the field? Did I unknowingly brush up against someone? Did I say something?

I came up with nothing. I then questioned whether or not I made a comment that offended the main female anchor, who sat at the desk right next to mine. These baffling questions continued with both my attorney and the paralegal as we waited for more information from the investigator. I had no idea what I had done to warrant this suspension. This was driving me crazy. I called coworkers and former coworkers who I thought may have an inside track. No luck. No one admitted to knowing anything.

About a week into my suspension, the woman investigating the complaint reached out to my attorney, and they agreed to a time and date at my attorney's office where I would be interviewed.

On May 18, 2018, I sat in the break room at my attorney's office, and the independent investigator, hired by the station, slid two pieces of paper to me. One of a meme of an African Proverb and the other, the front page of a TheGuardian.com article entitled, "How White Women Use Strategic Tears to Avoid Accountability." Two things I shared on my personal Facebook page earlier in the month. My Facebook page was set to private.

The meme said, "A child who is not embraced by the village will burn it down to feel its warmth," which, in my mind, was clearly from the movie *Black Panther*. A fact I was more than happy to explain to the white female investigator hired by the station.

Looking at the pieces of paper, I briefly smiled, thinking, "Oh, this is it. This is nothing. I can explain."

The interview with the investigator lasted more than an hour. I answered her questions truthfully and candidly. I had nothing to hide. I honestly thought the contents of Ruby Hamad's article were interesting and thought-provoking. I knew in my heart, mind, and soul that there was no reason for anyone to be offended by or mad at me because of the personal lived experiences of other women of color. I mean, surely, we all believe these women can share their stories. And surely, we believe that as a journalist and a woman of color, I can legitimately find value in those unique stories and experiences. I knew without a doubt that I could help the investigator and my white female accusers understand why there's no reason for anyone to be offended by a meme and an article written by a woman of color in Australia. Surely.

On June 12, 2018, I received a call from the station's HR director asking me to meet at a hotel located on the Country Club Plaza, a high-end shopping and residential area in Kansas City. I asked if I was going to be fired. He refused to answer. I arrived a few minutes early and anxiously awaited my attorney's arrival. Within minutes of sitting down in the hotel lobby, the HR director greeted me and escorted me back to a conference room. I told him that my attorney was coming. He informed me that as a station employee, I had no right to legal representation and that my attorney would not be allowed in the room.

I entered the room, sat down, and the general manager began reading from a piece of paper. I would soon learn that that piece of paper was my termination letter, better yet, my nonrenewal letter.

41 Action NEWS

June 7, 2018

VIA HAND-DELIVERY
Lisa Benson Cooper
6026 Euclid Ave.
Kansas City, MO 64130

RE: Confidential Notice of non-renewal of the August 6, 2017 Anchor Multi-Media Journalist
      Employment Agreement

Dear Lisa,

On August 6, 2017, you and Scripps Media, Inc. d/b/a KSHB-TV ("the Station") entered into an Anchor Multi-Media Journalist Employment Agreement (the "Agreement"), which outlined the terms and conditions of your employment. As you may recall, the Agreement expires on September 1, 2018.

Please be advised that the Station will not exercise its Section 7 option rights in the Agreement. Two coworkers recently complained of your conduct and an outside investigation was conducted by a third party, Ann Molloy, an attorney with Encompass Resolution, LLC in Kansas City. The Station has made the business decision to not renew your Agreement based on Section 8 of that Agreement and the findings in investigator Molloy's June 5, 2018 investigation report (the "report"), which, in part, outlines a violation of the principles of the social media policy. Your reporter position requires you to use social media effectively and appropriately and you were trained on the social media policy and reminded of the importance of your special responsibilities as a journalist.

Your recent social media postings made broad, unfair characterizations of white women as a group based on their race (white) and gender (female) and inappropriately associated such opinions with the Station. As your coworkers indicated as part of their complaints, your postings inappropriately conveyed that white women, as a group, behave differently than black women and suggests a bias toward a particular group which undermines the role of a journalist at KSHB to serve the entire community in a fair and balanced way. Further, your postings around the same time made reference to "burning down a village" without context which is also an inappropriate message for you to associate with the Station on social media. You identified yourself on Facebook as a journalist at both KSHB-TV and The E.W. Scripps Company and posted photos of yourself at the anchor desk with coworkers. Your social media conduct could be seen as an endorsement of the contents of the postings by the Station in the eyes of the Station's viewers and employees. The investigator also determined that you were disingenuous as part of her interview of you during her investigation. Such conduct, at minimum, is inflammatory, divisive, and inappropriate for a journalist who has an obligation to be fair and unbiased in her job and report the news based on facts to the entire community, particularly in these divisive times.

1

EXHIBIT _____A_____

SCRIPPS

When he got to the part about unfiled tax returns on page 2, I remember interrupting him and informing him that my husband had filed all of our back taxes in hopes of somehow changing the outcome. The general manager quickly responded, saying, "They were not filed as of the day of your deposition." He then continued reading the letter.

I was numb as the human resources director explained when my health benefits would end and reminded me once again that I'm not allowed on property. Again, I pushed back, "Can I come get my things?"

"No," he replied. "We'll catalog everything at your desk and ship your things to you."

I asked for a copy of the letter before leaving the meeting, which lasted less than five minutes. I greeted my attorney in the hotel lobby. After alerting him of my termination, he honestly appeared more shocked and riled than I was. He was stunned that such a simple act of sharing an article and a meme on Facebook would cost me my fourteen-year career.

Somehow, I was disappointed by the actions of my now former employer, but not surprised.

We left the hotel lobby and headed to my attorney's office to discuss KSHB-TV's most recent maneuver and to plan our next move.

CHAPTER 6

Unemployed and Offended

In the end we will remember not the words of
our enemies, but the silence of our friends.

—Martin Luther King Jr.

Unemployed and offended, that's how I started my journey as a former journalist of KSHB-TV. My fourteen-year journey at the NBC
affiliate in Kansas City, Missouri, had come to an end. As part of
the "nonrenewal" decision, the station agreed to release me from my
noncompete, which meant I could work at the competing stations in
Kansas City. However, with my highly publicized lawsuit, I doubted
that I would be an attractive candidate to the competition. The local
newspaper did an article about my suspension after the author of the
"White Tears" article Ruby Hamad, publicly denounced my suspension and termination on Twitter. People knew about my case, and
they were talking and tweeting about it.

Nonetheless, I started applying for television jobs and others positions. I didn't get so much as a response from television corporations.
I had no choice but to accept that my television news career was over.

I started adjusting my résumé and my LinkedIn profile to
become more attractive to other industries. Instead of using the title
of news reporter, I change it to communications specialist, in hopes
of non-newspeople understanding what I had done for more than
twenty years of my life and believing I could be an asset to their
company.

As I started my journey to a new career, I also had a strange experience of truly possessing my own time. For the first time in my life, I got up each day and pursued my own interests. Those interests, of course, included getting my boys dressed, fed, and off to school. After that, somehow, I had a renewed energy to find healthier recipes that my family would enjoy, and I miraculously went to the gym most days. I knew I wanted to live a healthier lifestyle. Now I had the time and the power to spend my time achieving my goals. It's crazy how awkward it is to decide how you're going to spend your day versus simply doing what you're supposed to do. I mean, I definitely valued my career as a general assignment reporter, but overtime, with the lack of opportunity and advancement, I had gotten to the point where I was disengaged and was doing what I needed to do and what I was expected to do. In truth, this behavior had smothered my desire to live my truth and pursue my authentic interests. Somehow, me being terminated brought that painful reality into full view.

My termination also made me extremely curious about why my now former coworkers were so offended by an opinion piece written by someone else about white people and systemic racism. As a black woman who worked in the media, I was all too familiar with seeing black people and people of color portrayed in a less-than-favorable light. I could not understand why my coworkers took the words of Ruby Hamad in her "How White Women Use Strategic Tears to Avoid Accountability" article as a personal attack on themselves. If they did not display the actions noted in Hamad's work, why were they offended? I did not understand, but I needed to understand so I could accept the outcome of the company's decisions and move forward.

I immediately started reading books, attending seminars and discussions about race, racism, anti-racism, system racism…anything that could help me understand my consequences. Kansas City mayor, Sly James, started a public series entitled, "KC Race and Equity Initiative." I sat through the first event, which was moderated by a former coworker and covered by my former station. It was a matter-of-fact candid presentation from an Asian woman about racism, white privilege, and systemic racism. Needless to say, I was hooked.

Throughout this series, I could not believe a room full of people of different racial, education, and socio-economic backgrounds were willing to sit through forums on institutionalized racism. The moderator Pakou Her defined racism, highlighting the importance of the misuse of power and went on to explain acronyms that I had never heard of, such as IRS and IRO, which were acronyms for "internalized racial superiority" and "internalized racial oppression." As the moderator eloquently spoke about the terms and how they played out in society, you could feel the discomfort growing in the room. To my surprise, no one walked out, and she continued to speak with authority and assurance that this was information that we all needed to know, understand, and utilize in our lives. I wanted to know more. I needed to know more. This knowledge was connecting dots in my mind regarding my termination and experiences in my professional and personal life.

My need to know more about these fascinating racial dynamics lead me to Robin DiAngelo's book entitled, *White Fragility*. The author of the article I was terminated over, Ruby Hamad, encouraged me to read it after I told her about my situation. Shortly thereafter, my attorney anonymously received two copies of the book in the mail and lent one to me.

The information in DiAngelo's book was enlightening and convincing. Immediately, I could attach her revealing words to the reality of my termination and my experiences of "good but not good enough" as an employee of E. W. Scripps. It also helped make sense of my May 2015 suspension for the tone of my voice. During that exchange, I believed my supervisor and I were discussing our opposing viewpoints about my decision not to use file video in a story about flooding, really no big deal seeing as I did as she requested by including the file video in my five and six o'clock live shots. However, in the subsequent letter that alerted me to my two-day suspension, I learned that my supervisor found my conversation to be "combative and disrespectful." Station leadership didn't even talk to me during the investigation, but based on her account of our conversation, I was suspended for the "tone of my voice." In the letter, despite having nothing else in my personnel file, my news director wrote that this was my "final warning," and any further issues could result in my termination.

An experience that made more sense after reading DiAngelo's book. In her eighth chapter entitled, "The Result: White Fragility," she wrote,

> By employing terms that connote physical abuse, whites tap into the classic story that people of color (particularly African Americans) are dangerous and violent.

In the same chapter, she also noted,

> White fragility functions as a form of bullying; white fragility keeps people of color in line and "in their place." In this way, it is a powerful form of white racial control.

After returning to work in May of 2015 following my two-day suspension, I remember being consumed with fear and obsessed with controlling the tone of my voice while at work. I was so afraid that fighting for a story or defending my work in the wrong "tone" would cost me my job. It was paralyzing as a journalist to always be consumed with how your superiors would interpret not your words but the tone of your voice.

DiAngelo's chapters also highlighted, "Racism and White Supremacy," "Racial Triggers for White People," and "White Women's Tears." I could not believe this white woman was spilling the tea on the how white people viewed race and loathed conversations about racism. In her book, DiAngelo warned,

> "The smallest amount of racial stress is intolerable—the mere suggestion that being white has meaning often triggers a range of defensive responses." She continued, "I conceptualized this process as white fragility. Though white fragility is triggered by discomfort and anxiety, it is born of superiority and entitlement."

My reading of DiAngelo's words soon lead me to book discussions and authentic conversations. I was so eager to be around other people who not only possessed this knowledge but were willing to have these difficult conversations. I now had a greater understanding of how the words of an article that I didn't even write could anger my two white coworkers to the point where they told management that they believed it was a "fireable offense."

Discovery Reveals Proof

My termination resulted in my August 2018 court date being pushed back to January 2019. It also meant another round of depositions and grabs for evidence, better known as discovery. Through discovery, we were able to get the report from the internal investigation and the notes the investigator took while talking to the interviewees. The investigator compiled more than eight hundred documents that included her notes of our conversation. I told her that I shared the article on Facebook so that my sister could see it and to get back to it because I wanted to watch the video on a larger screen and finish the article beyond the video portion. She didn't believe me. She noted in her report that I was disingenuous. At this point, I had no idea why this woman would call me a liar, seeing as I had and continued to maintain that there was nothing, in my opinion, wrong with the article. But nonetheless, the investigator decided I was untruthful, and station management took her opinion as their truth. In fact, me being disingenuous during her investigation also made its way into my nonrenewal/termination letter.

The discovery documents also included the names of the complaining white female coworkers, the text messages, and e-mails from them to management the day before my suspension.

Jessica McMaster, the investigative reporter, was the first to see my Facebook post and report it to management. I had already suspected her involvement because she stopped talking to me after being deposed by my attorney in my racial discrimination case. Despite having less on-air experience and no investigative unit experience, she was hired for the investigative reporter position that I applied for in 2015. Her text messages to the human resources manager gave some insight into her mind-set.

Jessica's Text Message to the HR

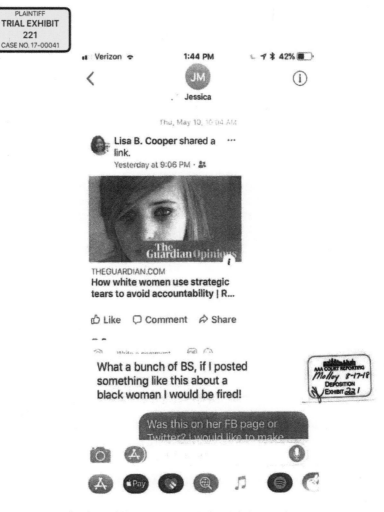

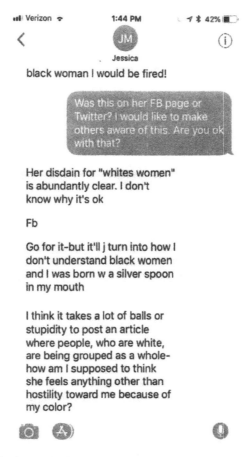

Jessica told the jurors she showed one of the main anchors, Christa Dubill, the article from my personal Facebook page because she was offended by it and wanted to get someone else's reaction. She admitted in court that she didn't seek the reaction of a person of color at work but didn't say why not. While in court, Christa said she took the time to think about my Facebook share before calling the company's EthicsPoint hotline to launch a complaint. She said despite having the option to complain anonymously, she wanted to use her name. So she did.

The operator created this report as Christa was sharing her disapproval of the article and me sharing it on my personal Facebook page. The operator typed that according to Christa, "Since January of 2018, Lisa, an African American woman, has been very hostile towards white women at work."

Christa's EthicsPoint Report

From: Giles, Dave
Sent: Friday, May 11, 2018 8:10 AM
To: Wright, Danyelle <danyelle.wright@scripps.com>
Subject: RE: KSHB

Reporter contact information
Reporter anonymous: No
Reporter first name: Christa
Reporter last name: Dubill
Phone number: 816-500-3465
Email address: christa.dubill@kshb.com
Contact availability: anytime
Case Information
Please identify the person(s) engaged in this behavior: Lisa Benson/Cooper - reporter
Do you suspect or know that a supervisor or management is involved? Do Not Know / Do Not Wish To Disclose
Is management aware of this problem? Yes
Please identify the nature of this discrimination or harassment, include all that apply: race and gender
Where did this incident or violation occur? 4720 Oak St
Kansas City, MO
64112
Please provide the specific or approximate time this incident occurred: Since January 2018
May 9, 2018
May 10, 2018
How long do you think this problem has been going on? 3 months to a year
How did you become aware of this violation? I observed it
Have you confronted the person engaged in this behavior? No
Details: Since January 2018, Lisa, an African American reporter, has been very hostile towards white women at work.

On May 9, 2018, Lisa posted an article on her Facebook page titled, "How white women use strategic tears to avoid accountability." On May 10, 2018, Christa saw the Facebook post and felt that it was very inappropriate. Christa feels that Lisa is grouping white women into a category of weakness and that is not right. Christa reports that Lisa is currently suing the company for racism. Christa would like Lisa's behavior to be addressed, especially because Lisa is a reporter and she could offend not only colleagues, but the community as well.

Dave Giles
513-977-3891 | dave.giles@scripps.com
SCRIPPS

From: Wright, Danyelle
Sent: Friday, May 11, 2018 7:59 AM
To: Giles, Dave <dave.giles@scripps.com>
Subject: RE: KSHB

Hi, Dave,
Will you send over or cut and paste the allegations?

Danyelle S.T. Wright,
VP, Employment and Labor Law, Chief Diversity Officer
The E.W. Scripps Company

Both of the women said in court that they knew I was working the day they saw the article, which would have been May 10. Both also said they did not think it was their responsibility to talk to me about the article or their disapproval of it. On May 11, while at home on personal time off, the HR director called me and told me I was being suspended for creating a hostile work environment based on race and sex. He refused to tell me anything more. Again, at this point, I had no idea what was going on, but I had no doubt that KSHB-TV's decision had everything to do with my pending lawsuit and my racial discrimination complaints against the station.

CHAPTER 7

Trial Preparations

The ongoing trial preparations included never-ending e-mails, sub-poenas, and a lot of questions about my husband not filing our taxes in a timely manner. I found out that he hadn't filed our joint returns since 2012, shortly before his December 2017 deposition. As a self-employed small business owner, I knew itemizing was time-con-suming for him, and I had seen the trash bags full of receipts to prove it. Naturally, I was upset at his procrastination, but I knew my taxes were being withheld from my paycheck, so no big deal, right? Wrong. To my surprise, in my June 2018 termination letter, the station also stated that it learned, during my husband's deposi-tion, that he had not filed our tax returns in a timely manner. At that point, I had no idea how my confidential tax returns had anything to do with my employment or my discrimination case, but clearly, they had become a factor. This was despite the fact that the station never mentioned them to me, following my husband's deposition, in which the station's general manager was present. I even told the GM before they fired me that my husband had filed all of the returns (thanks to a lot of yelling and screaming on my part). But that did not affect their decision to end my employment and include my taxes as a reason why.

During our ten-year marriage, my husband opened real estate-re-lated businesses and named me as a registered agent on some of them. As a self-taught, self-employed entrepreneur, there were a lot of mis-takes and a lot of redundancy. His novice business filings sent the sta-tion's attorneys on a desperate hunt to find outside income to prove that I was working for my husband while working for the station without written permission. They served subpoenas to my husband multiple times and threatened to physically search his business office for further documentation. This, in addition to serving a subpoena to Commerce Bank for bank records. They were trying to prove that I was actively working for my husband's businesses and getting paid. As a black man, he was extremely intimidated by the sheriff's deputies knocking at the door and serving papers at our personal home and at his business office. Nonetheless, he had nothing to hide. All their efforts turned up nothing. I was a full-time employee at KSHB-TV who simply wanted the same opportunities for advancement that my white coworkers enjoyed without the fear of retaliation.

Coworkers Deposed

Throughout the discovery portion of my case, I had attended a number of depositions for my racial discrimination trial, which included interviews of my news director, my general manager, and the human resources director. But now, with the new wrongful termination and retaliation charges and the new witnesses, new depositions were being scheduled.

As you may know, depositions are the opportunity for the attorneys to get sworn testimony from witnesses before trial. But for me, it was a chance to face my accusers for the first time. Both Christa Dubill and Jessica McMaster were questioned in the boardroom of my attorney's office in late 2018. Neither spoke to me as they took their seats and put on their microphones for the videotaped interview by my attorney. I literally stared in their faces the entire time. I didn't want to miss a word. I needed to know why their disapproval of my evening reading material and me choosing to share it on *my personal* Facebook page should have cost me my career. I definitely had my listening ears on. At this point, the station had hired attorneys for each woman in addition to the lawyers representing the station. I was nothing short of amazed at the money they were willing to pay in legal fees, but not in salaries.

During Jessica's deposition, she recounted how she saw the article on her Facebook feed, showed it to Christa who was sitting in an edit bay, and thought it was clearly how "Lisa felt about me." She also told my attorney how the article itself "categorized white women in a negative light." Surprisingly, she admitted that after being deposed by my attorney the first time, she stopped talking to me at work, and that the lawsuit had started causing "tension" in the newsroom.

Jessica appeared to fight back tears when she said that she was sad when she found out I was not coming back to work. I was confused by her emotional display surrounding my termination, seeing as I'd already seen the text messages she sent to the HR director and the e-mail from the general manager that appeared to be an ultimatum from Jessica, demanding my termination. According to the general manager, Jessica told him "she's tired of the toxic environment that Lisa has created, and she's not sure if she wants to continue working here and being subjected to it."

GM's E-mail about Jessica

PLAINTIFF
TRIAL EXHIBIT
289
CASE NO. 17-00041

From: Watt, Stephen
Sent: Thursday, May 10, 2018 3:47 PM
To: Winkler, Scott <Scott.Winkler@KSHB.com>; Wright, Danyelle <danyelle.wright@scripps.com>; Giles, Dave <dave.giles@scripps.com>
Cc: Fernandez, Ed <Ed.Fernandez@scripps.com>
Subject: Re: Lisa Benson Facebook page Screen grab - May 9 - Attorney Client Privilege - confidential

And as you were meeting with Christa, I was meeting with Jessica McMaster who is also very upset right now.
She wants to know why the company is letting her do whatever she wants, in her opinion.
She said she posted an article that was disparaging about black women she would be fired.
She said she's tired of being subjected to the on-going toxic environment that Lisa has created and not sure if she wants to continue working here and being subjected to it.

Steve Watt
Vice President |General Manager
41 Action News | 38 the Spot
4720 Oak Street | Kansas City, MO
D: 816 932-4110
Email: stephen.watt@KSHB.com
http://kshb.com | http://www.38thespot.com

During Christa's deposition, she recounted four reasons she had a problem with the article and found it offensive. I can't remember the reasons, but this list was clearly well rehearsed.

And for the first time, I heard of an incident where Christa attached the tears of our white female news director to me. She told my attorney about an incident when our news director was crying in her office and called Christa in to talk. During that private conversation, the news director attributed her red face and tears to me, following a conversation she overheard in the restroom. Without ever talking to me about it, Christa immediately sided with the news director who blamed me for her tears, and she went on to tell my attorney that after that she was "done" with me. Again, I knew nothing of the tears or of Christa's newly discovered disdain for me, but her deposition helped me understand why a woman I had worked with for more than a decade would believe I should be fired for sharing an article that she didn't approve of on my personal Facebook page. It was becoming painfully clear that her connection with her white female boss meant she had to oppose me—the black woman who was suing the station and making other white people uncomfortable. It was all starting to make sense. This had nothing to do with the article but everything to do with them working in solidarity to get me out of the newsroom so they can have a comfortable place to work.

When my attorney moved on and asked her specifically about the contents of the article and the "White Tears" phenomena, she said she couldn't recall the details of the article. During the deposition, she proceeded to read the article in her attempts to answer his questions. In my opinion, this was clear proof that she had never bothered to read the article with the intent of understanding the experiences of these women of color. She clearly scanned the article to validate her personal offenses at the title and the picture, and she felt her personal perception was reason enough to use her power, privilege, and position in the newsroom to get me out.

Both of the women were clearly taken aback at being named and outed in the discovery portion of the lawsuit and dragged into my court proceedings. Jessica even told my attorney that she now felt like she was a victim of the lawsuit because of all the personal information she had to turn over to comply with federal law. I tried to understand their offense at now being a focal point in my case, which initially was about the discrimination and lack of promotion opportunities for me as a black woman. But seeing as they decided to interject themselves into my racial discrimination case and made it a retaliation case, I was going to do everything in my power to give them their day in court.

Despite not being in the newsroom, I was still getting information from some current employees and distance and shade from others. While working in the newsroom, I noticed that some employees distanced themselves from me, but others still honored the friendship that had grown over the past decade. This was clear as I was still being invited to barbecues, kid's birthday parties, and the countless conversations at my desk. Now that I was out of the newsroom, it became painfully clear that my coworkers, black and white, wanted the station to know beyond a shadow of a doubt where their loyalty lied. I don't know if I did anything personally to offend these former coworkers, but it was clear that our relationships had changed. I had no choice but to accept this truth.

A number of my former coworkers were added to the witness list because their experiences in the newsroom somehow intertwined with my grievances against the station. Those people included a black female weekend anchor who was cursed out by her immediate white male supervisor, who somehow, despite being in earshot of management, was not suspended for the tone of his voice. And the white female morning anchor who was successfully promoted through the ranks after starting as a reporter, just like me. While my former coworkers may not have seen the correlation between their experiences at KSHB-TV and mine, my attorney did, as did the courts, so they had no choice but to surrender to depositions or to show up in court and testify. Needless to say, conversations, text messages, and calls from those and other former coworkers ceased. I was sad, and it hurt my feelings to be cut off from friends and women whom I thought were my friends. These feelings were intensified by the fact that we spent years talking about marriage, husbands, pregnancies, miscarriages, and careers. Despite the loss, my resolve for my voice to be heard and to finish this conversation with my former employer remained. And my commitment to Christa and Jessica getting their day in court only intensified as we moved closer to January 28, 2019.

CHAPTER 8

Trial Begins

The morning of Monday, January 28, I had very little sleep. I was consumed with worry about over sleeping and being late for jury selection in my own trial.

I felt confident walking into the federal courthouse. I climbed the stairs and turned over my phone to security officers before taking the elevator to the seventh floor in Judge Beth Phillips' courtroom. After covering court cases for years, I paused at the gallery of the courtroom and quickly proceeded beyond the small gate and to the plaintiff's table—my table.

The jury pool included more than forty people, including a handful of black people. None of the black people made it on the jury. The jury of my peers included seven white people and one Indian man. The gender was a fifty-fifty split, four men and four women.

My attorney's opening statements were concise in my mind. A synopsis of what I experienced at KSHB-TV. The defense's opening statement felt like a nursery rhyme of lies and half-truths. The defense attorney tried to convince the jurors that me being offered multiple reporter contracts to stay on the weekends was a decision made by the managers based on my performance and qualifications. He clearly wanted the jurors to believe that I should have been grateful to have a job and that my superiors did everything in their power to make me a better reporter, and it clearly didn't work. Hence, the lack of promotion and not being eligible for a Monday through Friday dayside shift. He never mentioned my fourteen years of experience or the accolades I received for my work.

The shocking part of the defense's opening statement started when he broached the feedback session over the use of file video that lead to my two-day suspension in 2015.

He told the jurors that the manager was trying to "manage as managers do, and Ms. Benson became hostile, upset, and aggressive." I was shocked because these descriptors were worse than the words used in the suspension letter, which were exaggerated when they were written in May of 2015.

Later in the hour-long opening statements, the defense referred to me as "angry" several times, accused me of yelling at my bosses, and rolling my eyes during conversations with my superiors. I couldn't believe it. It was like he was narrating a scene from a TV housewives reality show—the classic loud, angry black woman. However, the devastating blow came from the general manager Steve Watt's words. Watt is a white man who admitted that he had never had a conversation with me since being hired in 2017.

The defense attorney said, in opening statements, that Mr. Watt was aware of the anger I had for the company, and he believed the *Black Panther* meme on my personal Facebook page was directed at the company. Watt testified and the attorney highlighted in opening statements that he had received information from an unnamed source that I wanted the news director's head on a "fucking stake," and based on this knowledge and what he knew about me, he couldn't take any chances with workplace violence.

All this from a general manager who admitted to never having a conversation with me, ever. Not when he was hired, not at the countless station meetings, and not when he heard rumors of me wanting to decapitate my boss. Never.

As a black woman, I was used to hearing broad, negative characterizations about people of color in the news. What shocked me is that this multimillion-dollar media company, which I spent more than a decade working for, would use this tactic to describe me, a former employee. It was hurtful, irresponsible, and an outright lie.

The next day, in conversations while the jurors were not in the courtroom, my attorney, Dennis Egan, told the judge, "I'm not overstating it to say that yesterday the jury got to hear one of the most broad attacks on the plaintiff and her demeanor and interactions at work. I had no expectation that it would try taking it that far. I mean, you heard that there were threats of violence, that she is cursing and sarcastic and insubordinate." Thankfully, his lobbying the judge for the first witness, at that time current employee Dee Jackson, to be used as a character witness as well as a "me too" witness worked.

The first day of court and opening statements made me question whether or not the depictions of people of color in local news are as coincidental as I once accepted as the truth. I was watching as KSHB-TV and E. W. Scripps used that exact same story line in hopes of persuading the jury in their favor. Are news managers not doing the same when it comes to influencing viewers to believe a single story narrative that supports racism, negative stereotypes, and biases when it comes to black men in particular? By the end of opening statements, I was questioning how complicit I had been in supporting the single story narrative that paints black people as loud, angry, violent, and as something to be feared.

The judge released the jurors to go home for the day, following jury selection and opening statements. After instructions, the four men and four women got up and walked out of the courtroom. At this moment, I had no doubt that I had made the right decision in forcing my former employer to be accountable for my stagnant career and retaliatory dismissal. But I absolutely questioned whether or not I could convince this jury of my peers that I deserved an opportunity for growth, and I should still have my job. I definitely had my doubts.

First Witness Takes the Stand

Tuesday morning was cold and windy as I parked my car and marched up the stairs to the federal courthouse in downtown Kansas City. It was the first full day of testimony in my case.

After a lot of conversations between my attorneys and the two tables of lawyers in the courtroom for E. W. Scripps, the jurors were allowed to take their seats. A current KSHB-TV employee, sports anchor Dee Jackson, took the stand. Jackson had been at the station since September 2013. He too had filed a complaint against the station for lack of promotion opportunities and racial disparities. He testified to being passed over for the sports director position twice and an improper interviewing process that seemed to be created just for him. He handled himself well on the stand, and after the scathing depiction of me in opening statements, I felt vindicated when he talked about my interactions with coworkers in the newsroom.

He told the jurors, "Lisa has always been warm, welcoming, and friendly. I can recall recently, some of the last times that she was working, Lisa was pretty much the center of attention. She was, I don't want to say the life of the party, but she definitely had a crowd around her, and there were some interesting conversations being thrown around."

As he spoke, I fondly remembered the lively weekend conversations I would have with my former coworker friends. Despite it being just several months back, it felt like a lifetime ago. After I got fired and as the trial date grew near, some of those same people stopped talking to me. I wasn't invited to cookouts or get-togethers. In fact, some did not even speak to me when they passed me in the hallway at the courthouse. I understood that the trial had become an unfortunate inconvenience for the people who did not share my experiences at KSHB-TV. But I was shocked and honestly saddened at the coworkers who I thought were my friends who had become distant and even upset that my discrimination and retaliation issues had affected their real lives and their real workdays at KSHB-TV.

Before leaving the stand, Jackson told the jurors that when he was hired, he was the only black male there. He went on to explain that there were no African Americans in prime time at KSHB-TV. He defined prime time for the jurors as the five o'clock, six o'clock, and ten o'clock weekday newscasts.

Next up on day two was Lindsay Shively. She's a beautiful, friendly, all-about-business white woman with blonde hair from the Kansas City area. She was currently a morning anchor who had ascended through the ranks of being hired as a reporter in 2009. I honestly felt bad about Lindsay having to testify in my case. She and I had truly been work friends. I attended her housewarming when she bought her first home, danced at her wedding, and bought gifts for her baby shower. I'd even been to her parents' home. I truly felt bad about dragging her into my black people problems. Nonetheless, this was happening.

Shively testified that she informed the general manager that she wanted to grow into an anchor role, and she had started looking outside of the company. Shortly thereafter, in May of 2013, Shively was promoted to replace N. S. on the weekend morning show. N. S was a biracial female anchor, whom the general manager decided not to renew. In the fall of 2014, Lindsay was promoted again. This time, to replace weekday morning anchor J. S., an Asian woman who was demoted to the weekend anchor shift. Shortly thereafter, J. S. resigned and left the business.

Even while Lindsay was on the stand, we exchanged smiles and glances as she agreed that we were friends. I was worried that she thought my attorney was trying to say that she was unqualified for the promotions and opportunities. That wasn't the case. I hoped she realized that the question wasn't whether or not she was qualified. My attorney was trying to prove that I was too. I just wondered if she ever would believe that about me. Did she ever wonder why I was never offered a promotion? In her mind, after fourteen years of reporting and filling in on the anchor desk for E. W. Scripps, would I ever be ready for the anchor chair? Clearly, we all know now that the answer was no. But I couldn't help but wonder, as my white friend, did she ever wonder why Lisa, her black friend, was never good enough for the opportunities for advancement that had been available to her. Did she ever wonder?

Oh, the Hypocrisy!

Next up, Kent Chaplain, the digital director for KSHB-TV. He was responsible for digital media and social media as it relates to the station. His testimony initially should have been about social media policies and procedures. That all changed after his 2018 deposition when a member of my legal team found an interesting article on his personal Twitter page. The article that he freely shared via Twitter was an opinion piece from *The Guardian*, much like the one I was suspended over. The article he shared was entitled, "The NFL's Plan to Protect America from Witches." Remember, Chaplain is the manager who made and enforced social media guidelines. His sharing of this article proved that he didn't see a problem with sharing controversial opinion stories on social media.

Kent Chaplain, a white male, tried to explain to the jury why it was okay for him to retweet an opinion piece from *The Guardian* that made broad characterizations of NFL owners and women, but it was not okay for me to share an opinion piece about systemic racism.

The article he shared included a number of provocative lines from the author including, "He believed that the sexual desire men felt when looking at a woman who was not their wife was due to the vixen casting magic spells to tempt them. As punishment, these sexual sirens must be, if not beheaded, drowned, or hanged, at least fired from their cheerleading jobs."

My attorney forced Kent to acknowledge that sharing *The Guardian* opinion piece did not constitute his endorsement of all the opinions in the article. It was simply an interesting article that he chose to share on social media, which was much like my sharing of *The Guardian's* piece on "White Tears." He proved that I could read an article, find interest in it, and not be forced to agree with or endorse every thought written by another journalist. This was huge for my team because this forced the jurors to question why I was fired over an opinion piece when other employees, including the digital director, freely shared opinion pieces without punishment. My former digital manager didn't so much as look in my direction when he left the stand, but something in my spirit told me he knew he'd done me a favor by simply being his authentic self on Twitter.

General Manager Spreads Rumors

My general manager, Steven Watt, who'd been on staff for less than two years took the stand next. I was shocked when he detailed his educational experience as a bachelor of science degree in journalism. Listening to his testimony, I couldn't believe we both had bachelor degrees in communications, but I was still a reporter, and he'd climbed the corporate ladder and became the vice president / general manager of a media company. Wow! I couldn't help but wonder where would I have been had I been promoted within E. W. Scripps in the fourteen years I'd worked there?

One of the first questions my attorney asked was, "Am I correct in my understanding, Mr. Watt, that from the time you started in May of 2017 until the time of Ms. Benson's employment ended in September of 2018, the two of you never sat down and had a one on one conversation?"

Watt replied, "Not that I recall."

From there, my attorney introduced a series of e-mails and messages to and from Watt. One was the e-mail exchange from Christa Dubill to Steve Watt on the day they reported my Facebook page to human resources. Dubill told Watt she was upset with me for posting the article, and she was not sure how she would react when she saw me in the newsroom. Watt admitted that he cautioned her against talking to me, saying, "If you do that, Lisa will just turn it around and say you are attacking her."

I'd heard this before, during Watt's deposition, but I couldn't help but wonder what would have happened had we ran into each other in the newsroom that day. I can't help but think we would have had an eye-opening, thought-provoking conversation. Unfortunately, I was reporting in the field as Christa was running upstairs to the GM's office.

The e-mail exchange quickly turned to Jessica McMaster's reaction to the article. Watt said that McMaster told him that she's tired of being subjected to the ongoing toxic environment that Lisa has created. And she's not sure if she wants to continue working here and being subjected to it.

Watt later told the court that McMaster did not say "toxic" but changed the word to "tense" environment. He couldn't explain why he used the word "toxic" in relaying McMaster's story to the investigator. I have no doubt that his choice of words in May of 2018 impacted the company's decision to suspend me for creating a hostile work environment.

Watt admitted that according to KSHB-TV's social media policy, I did nothing wrong by sharing an opinion article because I didn't "like it" or make a comment. However, he went on to contradict himself and create an exception when it comes to stories about systemic racism.

He told the jurors, "There are nuances here when we're talking about different subjects. What she engaged in was offensive. It made unfair characterizations of white women as a group. It's not appropriate."

Apparently, racism, systemic racism, and the life experiences of people of color are offensive nuances that should not be shared on social media. I was both shocked and saddened by the blatant double standard and his lack of racial awareness or interest for that matter.

African Proverb

Watt's testimony eventually moved from e-mails to the African proverb that he spotted on my Facebook page after Jessica and Christa complained about the article. Watt was the first person to have a problem with the African proverb that read, "A child who is not embraced by the village will burn it down to feel its warmth." Despite not having one conversation with me, Watt immediately took it as a threat against the station.

From: "Watt, Stephen" <Stephen.Watt@KSHB.com>
Date: May 10, 2018 at 6:48:38 PM EDT
To: "Wright, Danyelle" <danyelle.wright@scripps.com>, "Giles, Dave" <dave.giles@scripps.com>,
"Fernandez, Ed" <Ed.Fernandez@scripps.com>, "Winkler, Scott" <Scott.Winkler@KSHB.com>, "Anderson,
Candace" <Candace.Anderson@scripps.com>
Subject: Additional post

Wanted to share this post as well. Obviously pointed to the newsroom also.

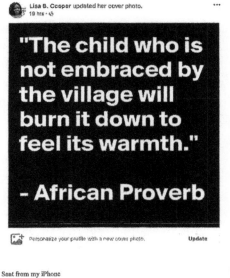

Lisa B. Cooper updated her cover photo.
19 hrs ·

"The child who is not embraced by the village will burn it down to feel its warmth."

- African Proverb

Personalize your profile with a new cover photo.   Update

Sent from my iPhone

Winkler
EXHIBIT NO. 280
10/17/18 DS
APPINO & BIGGS

1

Confidential Information—Subject to Protective Order

At this point, I had explained my interest in the Facebook meme numerous times. To me, it clearly was about the movie *Black Panther*. However, I was looking forward to hearing my former general manager's interpretations of my decision to share a meme on Facebook.

Watt told the jurors, "When I saw this post, I felt it was threatening."

He explained to the jurors that he was browsing my Facebook page looking for the article. He didn't see the article because my page was set to private but could see the African proverb. He told the jurors that he saw the proverb as proof of my mind-set when I posted the article, and he saw it as a threat to the newsroom.

He went on to say, "If the station is the village and we're going to burn down the village to feel its warmth, I feel that's a threatening statement."

Watt admitted he came to these conclusions about threats and violence without ever talking to me. Thanks to my attorney's questions, he had to restate that he had never had a conversation with me and did not attempt to talk to me about the meme or the article, ever. Thanks to a juror question, he had to admit that he lied, and the meme was not considered a threat of violence against the station.

He told the jurors,

> I didn't know her true intentions. I didn't really believe that there would be physical, a physical threat. But the comment was still provocative and threatening. And it to me pointed to her state of mind that there was a vindictiveness to what she was doing and so, that alone was a concern to me. But not to the point where we would need to involve law enforcement.

This was remarkable to me. A white man in a powerful, decision-making, career-changing position, who had never bothered to have a conversation with me, had already assessed my degree of vindictiveness based on a *Black Panther* meme. In his mind, I, as a black woman, was sitting at home on a Wednesday night plotting revenge against my employer instead of simply reading articles and playing around on social media after putting my kids to bed.

Watt later admitted that he told the independent investigator that he thought the African proverb was connected to the lawsuit. He told the jurors, following a question, "The lawsuit was filed in 2016, and so this has been a part of our lives for the last several years now."

Watt went on to talk about the decision to call me and inform me that I was being suspended for creating a hostile work environment based on race and sex and the company's decision to hire an outside investigator to look into the claims against me. After a lot of questions and objections from the defense counsel, Watt had no choice but to admit that the outside investigator concluded that I did not create a hostile work environment by posting the "White Tears" article.

Watt also told the court that he was the person who suggested to Christa Dubill that she could call the company's EthicsPoint hotline after she had already voiced her concerns to him and the HR manager. While answering a juror question, Watt admitted that without my lawsuit, corporate and the station's legal team would not have been consulted for a possible social media post violation.

Watt also told the court that he attended my deposition in May of 2017 when my nonfiling tax issue surfaced initially. He admitted to the jurors that between learning about the nonfilings of my taxes and my termination in June of 2018, he had never asked me about my taxes or informed me that my husband's procrastination could cost me my job. I believe this was a relevant point for the jurors because if this was truly a fireable offense, why didn't they fire me in May of 2017 when the tax issued was discovered?

The most shocking part of Watt's testimony happened when he talked to the investigator about an alleged threat someone supposedly overheard while I was talking on the phone in the parking lot. He told the investigator that he heard through the news director Carrie Hofmann, that Jessica McMaster told her that another employee told her, that I wanted "Carrie's head on a fuckin' stick."

Yes, this is thirdhand information, but nonetheless, the general manager of a television news station is testifying to it under oath in federal court. Watt admitted when he told the investigator, that he didn't actually hear me say it and didn't know who the unnamed employee was, nonetheless, he deemed this information credible.

"It was credible to me because Jessica is credible to me, and she told me that it was credible," said Watt.

Watt said he'd heard about the alleged threat six to eight months before my termination but admitted that he did nothing about it. Upon further questioning by my attorney, he had no choice but to admit that he did not perceive the rumored comment as a threat. Thank you, Steve Watt, for admitting there was no reason to believe that I was an angry, violent black woman outside of the company's attempt to manipulate this jury.

(Queen Bee) Christa D.

KSHB-TV main anchor Christa Dubill started working at the station in 2007, three years after I was hired. Not surprising to me, during depositions, she could not recall whether or not she or I was hired first.

Shortly after taking the stand, my attorney asked her about the day Jessica McMaster showed her the article and her mad dash to tell both the HR director and the general manager that she did not approve of me sharing the article. Christa went on to talk about her call to the EthicsPoint hotline. My attorney drew her attention to the report and a line that read, "Christa feels that Lisa is grouping white women into a category of weakness."

Despite reading it on the report generated by the EthicsPoint operator, Christa said, "I never felt like these were my words."

Then she went to say that she was offended by the picture and the title of the article right away because it showed a white women looking vulnerable and crying. She told the court, "The title and the picture and even as far as the summary under the title was offensive and grouped white women in a derogatory way by the color of their skin. So it was hard for me to understand how someone would find that inoffensive." She continued, "So it's less about the content of the article and more about the title and the picture."

Her testimony blew my mind. I got suspended, accused of creating a hostile work environment, and asked not to return to work because she did not like the picture and the title that another journalist attached to her work. Christa went on to admit to the jury that people, even people of color, have a right to write about, talk about, and share experiences in their lives, even if white people don't like them.

"I don't think the article was written fairly from my journalistic filter but there are definitely things said in that article that those people, that have an experience, have a right, in any situation, to talk about their experiences." She even added, "I understand how there are people that may feel the way some of those women described feeling."

Listening to her new interpretation of the article, I couldn't help but wonder again why was I fired? I agree. People can have experiences that are not my own, but my lack of knowledge or understanding does not negate theirs.

This conversation quickly went to Christa telling the jurors that I had made white women cry at work. Namely, the assistant news director, Melissa Greenstein, and the news director, Carrie Hofmann. Christa told the jurors, "The time that I'm thinking of with Carrie, she was blotchy-faced, and her eyes were watery, there weren't tears coming down."

Christa admitted that in all the crying incidents, there was no way for me to know these white women were crying over me.

Christa went on to say that she had not even seen the article on my personal Facebook page and that Jessica brought it to her attention while they were both at work. That very same day, Christa sent an e-mail to the HR director that read, "I can't help but think it would be a possible fireable offense if I or another employee was to post something like that about any group."

On day one of seeing the article on my personal Facebook page, this fellow journalist and mother of two boys immediately thought I should be fired—fired for sharing an article I found interest in. Why? Why should anyone be punished because she read an article that Christa didn't like?

Christa went on to talk about her disappointment in the independent investigator not fully sharing in her offense of the article. She told the court, "I feel like in that interview, she pressed me to have to make my case." She added, "I did not feel like she felt like my feelings were valid."

The witness testimonies were going long, and we were on a tight time period. Each side only had twenty-four hours to present its case because the judge had other obligations following our ten-day trial. So the judge asked the attorneys to start coming in at 8:15 a.m. to discuss topics so the jurors could be seated by 9:00 a.m. each day.

At the end of the day, I was mentally exhausted but, nonetheless, committed to seeing the trial to the end. Even in Christa's testimony, she had to admit that a person of color should be free to share experiences that are challenging to white people and their perceptions of racism.

The human resources director testified after Christa. Scott Winkler had been with the station for less than two years. Shortly after he started in April of 2017, I met him and had several conversations with him. He was such a (focused) listener that one could believe that he was actually understanding or even believing what you were saying. His deposition and his interview with the investigator proved me wrong. He too had made decisions about who I was despite having conversations with me.

Winkler said he had more than twenty years of human resources experience but admitted that he'd never received implicit bias training or heard of the term "tone policing."

Tone policing is when people are told there's a "right" way to talk about experiences. It refers to when someone focuses on the way you talk about something rather than what you are actually saying. Prior to my termination, I sent him articles about tone policing because in addition to the May 2015 two-day suspension for the tone of my voice, my tone also came up in subsequent conversations and e-mails from my superiors. This constant tone policing made it virtually impossible to fight for a story in morning meetings or disagree with my superiors without fearing punishment.

Winkler went over a few e-mails I sent to him about differential treatment. One of the incidences I highlighted was that of a white reporter who made an on-air mistake but was still working a Monday through Friday shift. Shortly after a few e-mails, the news director changed reporter schedules and put two white reporters on the weekend and two people of color on the weekday shift.

He also talked about two times where profanity was aired. One because I edited a photographer's story and didn't catch the curse word on a man's shirt in the video. The second time was when a photographer attempted to cover up curse words on a website, and in sending the video back to the station, the cover-up fell off, and multiple curse words aired. I took responsibility for the first one because I was the final gatekeeper of the story. The second incident, in my opinion, was an attempt to find fault with me as I was suspended for three days, but the two photographers involved in the story were not.

Thanks to the prying questions by my attorney, Winkler had to admit that he all but ignored my complaints of differential treatment and instead told me in an e-mail, "It appears that you automatically assume that everything that happens in the newsroom that you don't like is the result of discrimination. And that Carrie and Melissa only have that in mind when dealing with you. Jumping to that conclusion makes keeping the lines of communication open very difficult. And I believe your conclusion is wrong."

My attorney pointed out that despite him admitting that I had raised concerns to him about differential treatment that there was no investigation launched, nothing was done. Unlike when two white women complained about an article, I shared on my personal Facebook page.

Winkler acknowledged the May 10 text message from Jessica McMaster, which was essentially the beginning of the end for me. It was a screengrab of the article on my personal Facebook page and an article he admits to not bothering to read before calling me and telling me I'd been suspended.

The text read,

> "What a bunch of B.S."
> "If I posted something like this about a black woman, I would be fired."

After an exchange with Winkler about making others aware of my Facebook share, Jessica goes on to text,

"Her disdain for white women is abundantly clear. I don't know why that's ok."

McMaster Text to HR

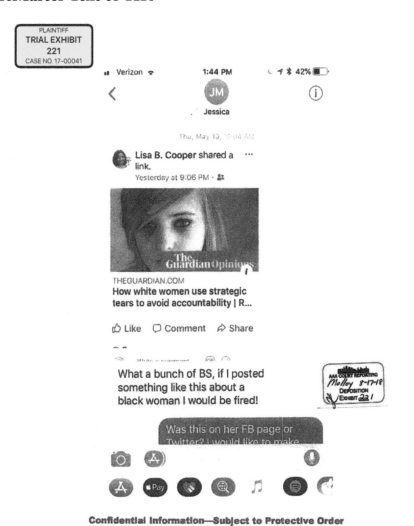

First of all, why does Jessica McMaster say I have a disdain for white women? And why didn't she have to explain her comment? What have I done to white women to demonstrate my disdain for them?

Then McMaster, after telling Winkler to "go for it," in regards to sharing this information with others, goes on to text, "It will just turn into how I don't understand black women and I was born with a silver spoon in my mouth." She then sent another text that read, "I think it takes a lot of balls or stupidity to post an article where people, who are white, are being grouped as a whole. How am I supposed to think she feels anything other than hostility towards me because of my color."

It still baffles me how this woman automatically assumed that what I read in the privacy of my own home, on my own time, has anything to do with her. Anything.

Watt went on to confirm Christa's e-mail he received on the same day about the article. It read, "Scott is this okay? I can't help but think it would be a possible fireable offense if I or another employee was to post something about any group. This is so upsetting."

Dubill E-mail to Human Resources

From:	Dubill, Christa <Christa.Dubill@kshb.com>
Sent:	Thursday, May 10, 2018 3:19 PM
To:	Winkler, Scott
Subject:	This is very concerning

Scott, is this okay? I can't help but think it would be a possible fireable offense if I or another employee were to post something about any group.

This is so upsetting.

It's hard to believe that the very day both of my white female colleagues read Ruby Hamad's article on my personal Facebook page, they thought a fair remedy was termination of my employment. They didn't suggest that HR talk to me, ask me to take it down, or force me to explain myself. None of that. They immediately wanted me to lose my career, lose my insurance, and lose my job. This further confirmed the othering that had taken place regarding me at KSHB-TV. Despite being a journalist, a wife, a mother, and a homeowner just like them, in their eyes, I was clearly something different—something that didn't deserve grace, understanding, or the benefit of the doubt. I couldn't imagine that they would want a fellow white working mom to lose her job for such a minor infraction. A white working woman would have been given the opportunity to explain, reevaluate, and self-correct, not me. From the girls to the HR director to the general manager, no one thought to call me and ask me to take it down. From day one, the plan was to figure out a way to get rid of me for sharing an article that they didn't like on Facebook.

On May 11, Winkler the HR director called me and told me there had been internal complaints that I was creating a hostile work environment based on race and sex. He didn't tell me who filed the complaints or any of the details. I distinctly remember being thoroughly confused. He didn't mention anything about Facebook or social media. In fact, I called him back a few minutes after to get him to tell me again so I could write down exactly what he said. He restated I would be suspended with pay as the allegations were investigated.

In relaying this phone call conversation to the investigator, Winkler said I was sarcastic on the phone and said I hung up on him.

The KSHB-TV employee he called in to witness the call contradicted his comments, saying he believed I hung up the phone because the call was over, which was in fact the truth. Surprisingly, the investigator caught the contradiction in his statement versus the witness, but he wasn't branded a liar or disingenuous. A word the investigator used to describe me, but she didn't have a lie to attach her opinion to.

Winkler went on to try to defend the retweet of Kent Chaplain's *The Guardian* article. He said because Kareem Abdul Jabbar was a public figure, it was okay to share his *The Guardian* article—a completely subjective stance that was not supported by station policy. An opinion piece is an opinion piece. Traditionally, as journalists, we're expected to explore knowledge and viewpoints beyond our own. I knew that professionally, I should not endorse others' opinions while covering work-related topics. But I had no reason to question my ability to read an article on my personal time, find interest in it, and share it on social media. Winkler was clearly rewriting the rules on the witness stand. Thankfully, the jurors caught on to his scheme.

Winkler told the jurors about the termination meeting at the hotel on the Country Club Plaza. I'll never forget my husband dropping me off at the hotel and my heart pounding through my chest. In my heart of hearts, I knew that I was probably being fired, seeing as they asked me to meet them off property, but I couldn't help but say a little prayer as I walked into the hotel lobby and took a seat. I arrived several minutes early and anxiously awaited the arrival of my attorney. Within minutes, I heard my name from across the room. I looked to my left, and Scott Winkler was waving me back to the conference room. When I entered the room, I told him and Steve Watt that my attorney was coming. They informed me that as a current employee, I didn't have a right to legal representation. Therefore, my attorney would not be allowed to sit in on the meeting. Watt took the lead on the talking points and informing me that my employment was ending while Winkler fielded my questions about insurance. Jeff Mulligan, the black executive producer who was hired after I filed my lawsuit, was in the room, but I don't remember him saying anything. There was a part of me that thought I would cry, but after years and months of walking on eggshells and weeks of being suspended and owning my own time, there was a piece of me that was ready to hear their story and watch the termination show. I sat there with legit questions and not a tear in my eyes. I was now even more committed to seeing how this chapter of my story was going to end. Bring it.

While testifying, Winkler also confirmed that I requested to come up to the station to pack up my desk and get my things. They told me that I was not to come on property. They informed me that they would pack up my items and send them to me. Immediately, I was devastated because I felt this was their second attempt to spite-fully end my television news reporting career by denying me access to the building to retrieve to my recent work and the ability to make a competitive résumé tape. I was heartbroken. This felt like the last nail in my career coffin. I'll never forget the four boxes that were FedExed to my home with the contents of my fourteen-year career at KSHB-TV.

Through the rest of Winkler's testimony, he talked about how my lawsuit came up during his conversations with the investigator, how Jessica McMaster was frustrated to be a part of the lawsuit, and how my news director, Carrie Hofmann's, sudden personal leave of absence was because of how stressed out she was because of my lawsuit. Hofmann went on leave while I was still at work. According to rumors, her mother wasn't doing well. I was surprised to learn that it wasn't a family crisis, but my lawsuit that initiated her break from work. I couldn't help but reflect upon the personal leave I took from KSHB-TV in 2015. I was clear that the reason I took the leave was because of the stress I was confronting each day in the newsroom and my pregnancy. My doctor prescribed me antidepressants as we talked about my new pregnancy and the realities of my job. Despite my doctor assuring me the drugs would not have an adverse effect on my child, I was not willing to risk it. So rather than showing up to KSHB-TV every day, drugged up just to conquer the day, seeing as my superiors were doing nothing to fix the toxic work environment that I had complained about numerous times, I took a leave of absence. It was unpaid, but I was so relieved to be away from work. The leave allowed me to get past the first trimester of my geri-atric pregnancy, seeing as I was thirty-nine years old, and room to breathe and gird myself up for the ongoing battle to keep my job at KSHB-TV.

According to Winkler, Hofmann was away for less than thirty days, so she must have returned after learning that I was on suspension.

Thanks to juror questions, Winkler admitted that no one inside the station even attempted to talk to me about the Facebook share; instead, they chose to launch a third party outside investigation. He admitted that was very rare, and the decision to do it was initiated by him, the GM, and station attorneys. He went on to say the article I shared had to do with white women and race in an unflattering and negative manner. I couldn't believe he said that, and others weren't bothered. As journalists, we know that we oftentimes do stories about people and communities of color, that are unflattering. So essentially, what I took from Winkler's dominant white male perspective is that an independent investigator was called because I dared to share an article that showed white women in an unflattering light. I couldn't help but believe that the jurors caught that distinction, seeing as they too are consumers of local news and its predictable negativity, especially when it covers communities of color.

Jessica McMaster's Testimony

From the sharing of her high school graduation date, Jessica McMaster's testimony reeked of white privilege. She graduated from high school in 2002, two years before I started my job at KSHB-TV. Nonetheless, there was no doubt in the minds of my white superiors that this woman, who initially pursued a nursing career, was more qualified. She told the jurors that she was a nurse's aide for ten years and switched careers. In 2012, she earned her bachelor's degree in journalism. In 2012, I was an Emmy Award-winning journalist at KSHB-TV with more than thirteen years of broadcast journalism experience. I had already worked in three television markets after graduating from college with a bachelor's degree in mass media arts. Nonetheless, in the minds of my white female bosses, I would forever work toward promotions that I would never be good enough to obtain.

Jessica spent a lot of time going back and forth with my attorney, trying to legitimize her lack of experience and validate her general assignment reporting experience as investigative unit experience. It was interesting to watch her carefully explain her credentials over and over again to my white male attorney who was ready to pick apart her experience and compare it to mine. He was carefully writing her words on a huge flip chart for the jurors to see. He wrote down, "Mostly day turns" to help the jurors understand that general assignment reporters do daily turn stories, not investigators as Jessica tried to paint herself as in front of the jurors. Later in her testimony, she told the jurors, "I was new to being a part of an investigative unit."

I don't know if my majority white jury understood the assault on my psyche after being told by my news director that I was not qualified for the investigative unit job because I had never worked in an investigative unit despite my years of experience. Nonetheless with her limited experience, Jessica was hired, and they believed in her ability to grow into the position.

Jessica also talked about how she didn't have to shoot and edit her own video despite signing an MMJ contract. An MMJ is expected to set up, shoot, write, and edit his or her own stories. The MMJ duties were bestowed upon reporters objectively by the supervisors. So in many cases, it was the black and brown employees who were expected to MMJ while the white reporters, much like Jessica, somehow avoided the oftentimes embarrassing realities of shooting your own video while trying to carry on an intelligent conversation with your interviewee. She told the jurors, "I would edit packages here and there, but we didn't do it consistently because we always had photographers. So it wasn't like I had become—I hadn't become very advanced at it."

This is one of the subtleties of racial inferiority in the newsroom. This was blatant inequality between whites and people of color in the newsroom. This behavior by management went unchecked due to contractual obligations; as employees, we were expected to simply do what we were told. The white employees, especially the women, were seen as soft, fragile, and something that needed to be protected and handled with care. Therefore, many white women were never burdened with shooting their own stories. The reverse was the case for women of color. Some of the black reporters were expected to MMJ every day, and others, like myself, were called onto to get video or do interviews for other white reporters. A difference of treatment and expectations that I brought to their attention, but contractually, they could do whatever they wanted regarding my schedule or work assignments.

Jessica went on to talk about the Adrian Jones story. Adrian Jones was a biracial seven-year-old boy who went missing from his Kansas City, Kansas, home in 2015. It was a day-turn story about a missing child. Police investigators soon discovered that the child had been killed and fed to pigs allegedly by his father and stepmother. Jessica did an extensive investigative piece on the child, and his unspeakable abuse after it had been covered several times as a day turn by a number of reporters, including myself. I did an MMJ story of a court proceeding where I interviewed the child's maternal grandmother, which was the station's first contact with her. Sometime after seeing my story, Jessica e-mailed me about the story, writing, "tear-jerker" and wanted to reach out to the grandmother herself.

This became an issue in the trial because as part of my petition for the investigative reporter job, I suggested to the news director, Carrie Hofmann, that we focus more on day turns and answering questions left in the minds of viewers to create must-watch investigative pieces. Essentially, that is exactly what Jessica ended up doing with the Adrian Jones' story. She created an investigative series out of a day turn, general assignment story about a boy who was killed by his parents. The point of it being part of the trial is that the station basically used my idea and allowed Jessica to capitalize on it. I could tell through her defensive testimony. She clearly thought I was trying to take credit for her work.

After defending her work on the Adrian Jones story, Jessica told the court that she "liked Lisa. We were friends." She even went on to agree that she found me to be polite, cordial, and professional. These were clearly characteristics my attorney wanted Jessica to confirm in hopes of counteracting the angry black violent woman narrative that was presented by the defense counsel in opening statements. After saying all this, she admitted that she stopped talking to me after being deposed for my discrimination case. By the time she saw the Facebook post, she told the jurors, "Lisa and I hadn't spoken for several months." My attorney asked her why she didn't sit down with me, and she confidently said, "We weren't friends at this time."

At no point in her testimony did our once existing friendship end. Even according to her words, the only thing that happened that impacted our relationship was her being deposed for my discrimination lawsuit. And I'd have to believe by her testimony that drawing her into my black people problem was simply offensive to her. It was okay that I had a discrimination lawsuit against the station; it was okay that she and I talked about it, and she would even appear to empathize with the fact that I'd never been promoted, or the fact that I was still on weekends. But I believe once my problems illuminated her privilege and exposed her own inadequacies, she was done with me. She had no interest in seeing or talking to me at work anymore. The discovery of her personnel files by my attorney appeared to be a tipping point.

"I thought personnel records and things like that were private, and so, yeah, when you walk into a room with attorney and your stuff is all out there, it was a little jarring." I don't think I was prepared for that." She continued, "I'm not being sued. I just took a job."

During my time on the stand, my attorney asked me about my relationship with Jessica. I told the jurors she was worried that her less-than-perfect performance as an investigator would impede her growth with the company. And since she was from Detroit and E. W. Scripps had a station in Detroit, she was expecting opportunities to come her way. I distinctly remember her telling me, "This is my real life, Lisa. This is my real life." Those would have been among the last words she ever spoke to me, as if my lack of opportunity at KSHB-TV wasn't affecting my real life.

To be honest, I completely understood her frustration with being dragged into my lawsuit, seeing as she simply got the job I wanted. I didn't understand why she didn't just speak her truth. To me, it's the equivalent to being a witness in a car crash. You're not the defendant, but your truth could aid justice. Who would not lend their truth to help someone else achieve justice when asked? Speaking her truth did not change her reality. She would still have the investigative position, working a Monday through Friday position, and making significantly more money than me. What was her problem? She clearly didn't hire herself for the position. I told the jurors, "She did nothing wrong. She took an opportunity that I wished I had an opportunity to take." In fact, I had even apologized to her for being sucked into my black people problems before she was deposed. She told the court that after being deposed, she wasn't mad at me, but she still couldn't explain why we suddenly stopped talking. And I remember waiting to hear about the deposition and her passing through the newsroom, never talking to me ever again.

While she testified that it hurt her when she found out I was not coming back, Jessica admitted to sending the text that said, "If I posted something like this about a black woman, I would be fired."

She also admitted to saying she sent Winkler a text that I had a "disdain for whites women." Along with "how am I supposed to think she feels anything other than hostility toward me because of my color."

As she was speaking, I did not understand how she arrogantly thought this article had anything to do with her. She went on to talk about how she sat in her office fuming over the article and then walked to an edit bay and saw Christa Dubill, the main anchor. She said she walked in and put the phone down just to get Christa's reaction. She said Christa put her finger up in the air and gasped, saying, "This is not OKAY."

At this point, I'm wondering, what's not *okay*? Is it not okay for me to read something you don't like? Is it not *okay* to share an article on social media that you don't like? What part of my personal leisurely reading has to be approved by my white coworkers? This was crazy to me, seeing as nothing about the article was directed at anyone at the station. These were all their personal opinions and assumptions that would fuel a white racial framework of solidarity and superiority that I had no way to combat. Jessica later said in testimony, "I felt like the article discriminated so I reported it to HR." She also said, "I just want them to handle it and I didn't want to have anything else to do with it."

And clearly, she believed that if she didn't like it, I should have known it, and I should have known that I could not share it. Jessica admitted to knowing that the woman who shared the article when it showed up on my Facebook timeline was a white woman. When pressed about her understanding of the "White Tears" phenomena, she said she'd vaguely heard of the concept but hadn't heard a ton about it before the article. When pressed further about her research into "White Tears," she said, "You can't just say there's 'White Tears' or 'white privilege' and then write something that seems pretty hateful and then just get it under that category to skirt that by." It appears that in Jessica's mind, anything that she does not agree with or identify with is discriminatory and hateful. Clearly, there is no such thing as opposing viewpoints or opinions on systemic racism or racial dynamics in the mind of this journalist. How sad.

She said repeatedly that me sharing the article was endorsing the article. This, despite the fact that the station's social media policy, says that we can share controversial topics; we just couldn't like them. In front of the jurors, Jessica doubled down on her own social media guidelines—that in her mind, I violated and discriminated against white women.

> "She shared the headline that was so offensive to me. She did it without comment, yes." She then added, "But it indicated to me that she was putting her support behind the idea, which she has since come out saying she does."

Again, the arrogance. Why does she get to rewrite social media policy, and how does she know what I support one way or the other? Because at this moment, as she addresses the court, no one at KSHB-TV had asked me about my feelings regarding the article, including Jessica.

My attorney went onto highlight her less-than-stellar performance reviews that did not impede her from being renewed and validated as a valuable member of the investigative unit. Her 2015 review read, "Jessica must find ideas for day-turn investigations. She is still struggling with the balance between digging and quick turns."

Day-turn investigations is exactly what I suggested to Carrie Hofmann in trying to be promoted into the investigative unit and what Hofmann is now expecting of the investigative reporter they hired over me. Under her first contract, McMaster made $65,000, which was more than $10,000 dollars, more than what I was making as an Emmy Award-winning journalist in the newsroom with more than a decade of experience with the company. I'm sure everyone on the corporate structure of E. W. Scripps did and will continue to attribute this inequality and lack of promotion for me to anything but race. But I have no doubt in my mind that if I were a white woman with my experience, going up against Jessica McMaster, I would have been the better candidate. When she was hired, she had ten years of nursing experience and less than three years of news experience!

The Good ONE

The black people at KSHB-TV always had a different vibe in the presence of each other versus the atmosphere when we were in front of our white coworkers or managers. For example, during my entire time at 41 Action News, there was one African American photographer who was younger in age but definitely beyond my years in wisdom and spirit. I literally referred to him as everybody's uncle. And in that unique and genuinely caring relationship, there were conversations we would only have in the live trucks or on the phone. I didn't realize then, but now it's painfully clear how much assimilating and white-centering we all did as people of color, working for KSHB-TV.

Dia Wall was a black female reporter/anchor hired into a reporter position in April of 2015. She and I had been friends at work. We shared husband chronicles, pregnancy stories, and more conversations about life in general than I can recount. Unfortunately, the burden of my lawsuit weighed heavy on everyone. She told the courts that the lawsuit allegations caused the distance in our relationship. I didn't fully understand, sitting at the plaintiff's table, what she was mad about, but I figured if she wanted me to know, she would tell me. And I had long accepted that this journey to answers and accountability for my stagnant career at KSHB-TV was going to cost me people whom I genuinely cared about and liked. Dia was one of those people. Nonetheless, I appreciated her sharing her truth, which in many ways proved the differential treatment at KSHB-TV that existed when it came to black employees versus white employees.

Within minutes of getting on the stand, Dia shared her media career with the jurors, from working with the Dallas Cowboys to a weekend anchor position in Sherman, Texas, to a morning show anchor in Tyler, Texas. Dia is a beautiful, talented reporter with a robust personality. Unfortunately, she was yanked into my lawsuit by the white male nightside executive producer who cursed her out in the middle of the newsroom but didn't even get so much as a written warning. This verbal attack on Dia happened after I was suspended in May of 2015 for the tone of my voice. I was suspended for merely discussing my decision not to use file video. To me and my attorney, this was a clear example of differential treatment.

Dia told the jurors about the conversations that lead up to the expletive-laden verbal attack against her by Sam Eaton, her white executive producer. Apparently, the story she was assigned that day was somehow related to the racial incidents and protests at the University of Missouri in Columbia. In those protests, students walked out and were demanding that the president of the university be removed from his position. Because of this racially charged event that made national news, local universities, including the University of Missouri in Kansas City, hosted student forums to engage their students on race relations on campus. Dia was told to cover the UMKC forum. She told the jurors there were less than two dozen students in attendance. She said that as the reporter, she immediately noted there was no angered students, no yelling, no emotion, just adults talking about race relations on campus. Dia and her photographer shot the video, did interviews, and returned to the station to regroup and find a story that could lead an evening newscast.

According to Dia's testimony, when she told the nightside executive producer, Sam Eaton, that there was no story there, he lost it. She told the jurors that he started a three to five minutes expletive-laden rant at full volume that included him saying to her, "Dia, do you want to fucking lose? Do you want to be a fucking loser? Do better. Are you a fucking loser?" She recounted the harsh words very matter-of-factly, but it was clear that they still bothered her.

As she spoke, anger and sadness welled up in my eyes. I had to wipe away tears as I watched this black woman recount a verbal attack that I already knew her managers and the company that claims to value her did nothing about. I told my attorney that this was so upsetting for me to hear because this further proves the lack of human value and decency that existed for people of color within this organization.

Within two years of being employed at KSHB-TV, Dia had received opportunities that were unavailable to me. The talented reporter/anchor was promoted to the weekend anchor position and given the chance to hobnob with corporate management as the station's leadership champion. I had no doubt that she was qualified to do the job, but I knew my lawsuit fueled the company to find a minority to fill the position that was vacated by a blonde-haired white female who'd unexpectedly left. So in her recounting the attack, the disturbing part for me was that even in valuing Dia as a woman of color, they refused to protect her basic humanity by requiring her superiors to give her the same level of respect that was automatically bestowed upon her white counterparts.

A personal observation on my part that Dia clearly didn't see. When asked about Sam Eaton's motivation for berating her in front of and in earshot of coworkers, including news director, Carrie Hofmann, and assistant news director, Melissa Greenstein, Dia told the jurors she didn't believe his behavior was racially motivated. She said she thought Sam was "just off."

She explained, "I in no way believe that it was racially motivated." She continued, "He just lost it. Like, the man was just off. I just think he's crazy."

When my attorney pried further regarding the station's response to Sam's crazy rant, Dia had no choice but to shed light on the obvious difference between how Sam was treated by management as a white man for clearly cursing her out and how I was treated as a black woman for disagreeing with Melissa Greenstein about the use of file video.

Dia told the jurors that Sam was not suspended and did not miss any work as a result of his verbal attack on her. Sam Eaton later testified in a videotaped deposition that he did not receive a verbal warning, a written warning, or a suspension. He admitted that despite the fact that Carrie Hofmann and Melissa Greenstein both heard the verbal attack, neither felt it warranted discipline.

In direct contrast to his verbal assault on Dia Wall, when Eaton yelled, screamed, and showed his "crazy" to a white male coworker the following year, he was quickly suspended and subsequently terminated.

During discussions with the judge at the bench, the defense counsel fought to omit Sam Eaton's deposition. The defense attorney told the judge that since Dia Wall did not complain about Sam's behavior personally, it was a moot point.

Thankfully, the judge disagreed. Sitting there listening to these discussions while the jurors were not present, I couldn't help but think about when Dia told me about the incident. While sitting at my desk, Dia told me how disrespected she felt after Sam cursed her, and that it was one of the lowest points in her professional career. Sitting in court, I couldn't help but wonder why she didn't complain to HR. But I quickly remembered the lessons I've learned through my own career at KSHB-TV, my unexpected termination, and my journey to the lawsuit. I remembered how much I tried to fit in and not make waves in hopes of climbing the corporate ladder at E. W. Scripps. I recalled how I thought my silence, empty smiles, and perfect assimilation with my white coworkers would help me further my career. While Dia and I never talked about her decision to remain silent, I couldn't pretend as though I didn't understand. I absolutely understood.

Dia Wall also discussed her promotion to the weekend evening position and her desire to get off weekends if that opportunity arose for her at KSHB-TV. She told the court that there were no African American prime time anchors at the station. She defined prime time for the jurors as the six o'clock, ten o'clock, and the morning show newscasts.

She also talked about the thirty-minute segment she did about the 1968 Kansas City Race Riots. My attorney showcased her work to outline how willing KSHB-TV was to share controversial viewpoints about race. My attorney showed a video from her story and highlighted certain quotes to further prove to the jury just how provocative and unnerving race stories on KSHB-TV had been in the past. One of the quotes my attorney highlighted came from our current congressman, Emanuel Cleaver II, who said, "Anybody who is satisfied with where we are is actually contributing to us becoming worse. Because the moment that we're no longer intentional about trying to improve race relations is the moment that we begin our reverse."

It was so crazy to see my former coworkers who would congregate at my desk and exchange travel, husband, and baby stories walk past me in the courtroom as if we don't even know one another. To be honest, it hurt a little more with Dia because she is a black woman, but this journey has also taught me that despite what the media tells us, black people are not monolithic. We too can have vastly different interpretations of the nation that we live in. After all, we have different backgrounds, lifestyles, and experiences that make us our own unique individual selves. So there is no reason to expect that Dia Wall, as a woman of color, feels anymore kinship to my journey to justice than my white colleagues. So my challenge moving beyond this chapter of my life is to give everyone their autonomy to be their authentic selves in my presence. In people being their genuine selves around me, I have the power and necessary knowledge to choose my friends among those who understand my quest for racial knowledge, equity, and accountability. Moving forward, my plan is to allow this to remain true regardless of the person's skin color. I believe everyone should be working to dismantle institutional racism, and shame on those who choose to ignore injustice in the interest of protecting their personal interests.

My White Expert

Early on in my discrimination case, my attorney, Dennis Eagan, commissioned the expertise of an implicit bias expert. Dr. Monica Biernat, a research psychologist, who taught at the University of Kansas. Among other topics, she researched and studied stereotyping, prejudice, and discrimination. When she took the stand, that was my first time ever seeing Dr. Biernat although I had heard her name countless time from my attorney. I knew she was white because I asked my attorney that shortly after he informed me that she would be used as an expert witness. I knew that bringing a black person in to talk about discrimination, implicit bias, and racial equity would be a moot point in a federal courtroom dominated by white jurors. We needed a white ally. Thankfully, my attorney knew the relevance of race without me even having to explain it.

But seeing her for the first time, I was further encouraged to see how regular-looking she was. She kind of reminded me of Robin DiAngelo. A normal brown-haired white woman. A woman I hoped could permeate the minds and hearts of my seven white jurors. Maybe they would look at her, identify on some level, and trust the words that were coming from her mouth despite the fact that she was there as my expert witness.

Biernat told the jurors that she had seen Ruby Hamad's "White Tears" article and confirmed that there's a long history of studying issues relevant to white denial of racism and white defensiveness when racism comes up. As she was speaking these words, I literally wanted to scream "yes!" and start pumping my fist in the air like I was at a basketball game, and my side just made the shot.

Biernat shared that "White Tears" came up as a topic of conversation among her academic circles around 2015, and since then, it's been routinely discussed among her peers and students. She told the jurors that white people might experience two kinds of threats in situations when they are confronted with systemic racism. One, a threat to meritocracy, which means maybe I have the things that I have, not because I earned them. And two, a threat to the morality of the group—someone is accusing my group of bad behavior, and I don't want to be identified with that negative behavior. She went on to say that the primary response to these threats for white people is denial, defensiveness, and turning this around on the accuser to talk about how difficult the conversation on race is making them feel.

Ding, ding, ding! Dr. Biernat hit the nail on the head, and I was ready to go home. It was clear to me that this is exactly what happened regarding my lawsuit and my posting of the article in the minds of my two white coworkers. How dare I, a black woman, complain about race discrimination and share an article about systemic racism and how it manifests in the relationships that exist between white women and women of color? How dare I expose them to the negative truth of racism and how they could be contributing to the problem?

Again, I thought Dr. Biernat's testimony eloquently explained my case and "White Tears," but I couldn't tell if the jurors agreed. Looking over at my panel of four men and four women, I could tell my story was resonating with the men. The women, I couldn't read. The two older white women seemed receptive, but the two middle-aged white women appeared agitated. I had no doubt that they too were offended by the article, and my attorney would have a hill to climb to convince them that sharing the article was not a fireable offense.

During Dr. Biernat's testimony, I briefly morphed into a student of race relations, something I had legitimately become in my quest for justice at KSHB-TV. Dr. Biernat explained to the jurors the historical reference of white women's tears and how they have been used as the grounds for punishment against black men. She brought up Emmett Till. You may recall fourteen-year-old Emmett Till was lynched in Mississippi in 1955 after being accused of whistling at a white woman in the Jim Crow era South.

Biernat continued saying that white tears can be dangerous to black people and how that fear and the dire reality of their power forces others to comfort the white crier in hopes of counteracting the looming consequences of those white tears.

The jurors didn't have any questions, and the defense counsel didn't really make any solid points on the cross-examination. But when Dr. Biernat left the witness stand, I questioned whether or not her familiar white face coupled with her brief explanation of white tears were enough to convince this jury that I should not have been suspended and ultimately fired for reading an article and sharing it on my personal Facebook page. To be honest, I was not convinced, but I had no choice but to keep hope alive because I was not going to give up or settle.

Former GM and KC News Jesus—Brian Bracco

I will never forget the e-mail that announced that Brian Bracco, KMBC Channel 9's former news director, was coming to KSHB-TV as the new general manager. As far as the anticipation and buzz in the newsroom, it was almost as if Jesus himself were coming to lead the charge to turn the station into the news leader in Kansas City.

When he arrived at the station, he seemed nice. People were walking on eggshells, trying prove they deserve to keep their jobs, me included. Seeing as I was a general assignment reporter hoping to grow into an anchor position, I was less worried about keeping my job and more focused on finally proving I'm ready for a promotion. Just like all the general managers and news directors before him, I was ready to prove and reprove that I deserved to be in the newsroom and had already earned an opportunity for advancement much like my white colleagues.

Bracco told the courts that race and diversity were a factor when it came to hiring as KSHB-TV, saying the staff should reflect the market. Bracco also talked about the turnover at KSHB-TV during his tenure across all departments. He credited the high turnover rate to the fact that KSHB-TV was a fourth-rated television station with declining revenue and terrible ratings. He said viewers were leaving KSHB-TV because they didn't like what they were seeing on air. He also added that people didn't like coming to work.

As he was talking about his time at 41, I remembered that Elizabeth Alex, Mark Clegg, and Christa Dubill were the main anchors at the station when he took over. I agreed with his assessment that people didn't like coming to work. A huge part of the problem was who station management and leadership at E. W. Scripps hired, including a white female news director that they hired a life coach for in hopes of helping her be nicer to employees. Yes, a life coach. But nonetheless, E. W. Scripps saw leadership in her and gave her the opportunity to prove them wrong.

Bracco went on to talk about the strides in the ratings that were made during his leadership, which was a little different than what he said to my attorney during his deposition, but nonetheless, they agreed that he benefited the station. Then it was time to talk about me. I told my attorney that shortly after starting as the general manager, Brian Bracco invited employees to schedule a sit-down meeting with him, and I did just that. During our meeting, I told Bracco that I loved working for KSHB-TV, and I was interested in growing into an anchor position. Because I was pregnant at the time, I followed our conversation up with an e-mail that included my résumé and a link to my work. I was hoping that he would see the not pregnant version of me and see me as part of his master plan to dominate local news in Kansas City.

During our conversation, I definitely didn't feel assured that my plan had worked. He seemed confident about his ability to make us number one and told me that "not everyone would be staying on" at the station. I didn't know how to take that. I definitely knew that I would have to prove myself as a strong reporter, yet again, but that didn't bother me. I knew how to report. At this point, I would jokingly say to friends I could package rainwater. What I didn't know is whether he saw me as a potential anchor. Nonetheless, I was going to put myself in position so he could see what I could do.

When my attorney asked him about our one-on-one conversation, he said he couldn't remember what he said to me. My attorney had to read excerpts from his December 2017 deposition to remind him that he did, in fact, remember telling me that.

Bracco went on to name some of the staff changes that took place shortly after he took over as general manager, and he hired Carrie Hofmann as news director. Those changes included an Asian American assistant news director being terminated and replaced with by a white male. Also, an Asian American morning anchor was demoted to weekends and a white female, Lindsay Shively, was ultimately promoted into the position.

Bracco then shared the private conversation he had with Lindsay Shively, where she told him that she wanted to grow into an anchor position. When she mentioned looking at other stations within the group, Bracco told her not to look elsewhere and committed to finding an anchor position for her. Shortly thereafter, the biracial weekend morning anchor was informed that she would not be renewed, and Lindsay was moved into her position. Lindsay had already testified to the courts that she never applied for the position; she simply made her interest in growing with the station known to the general manager.

This entire exchange, coupled with Lindsay's previous testimony, left me baffled. I too met with Brian Bracco and informed him that I wanted to grow as an anchor. I too had over the years asked for opportunities to grow within the Scripps group. Why was it that Lindsay's conversations actually warranted a change in her circumstances and mine did not?

Bracco went on to talk about other hires, including he and Carrie's decision, to hire a woman he described as ethnically ambiguous for the weekend morning anchor job after the Asian American woman who got demoted to the position quit and took a job out of the business. My attorney didn't have him explain what ethnically ambiguous meant, or why it was a desired feature for a potential anchor. But as a regular black woman, hearing him say that made me feel like the other, other. I knew that as a black woman, I would have fewer opportunities in the television news industry than my white counterparts. But now to hear this older white male, who was clearly in a decision-making, hiring position, further compartmentalize women of color was surreal. It felt like the unspoken racial hierarchy was screaming to me that it's more acceptable to be a woman of color when no one can figure out what you are. Ambiguous. And that was yet another hurdle I would never clear. Everything about my brown skin, my broad nose, and my full lips screams black woman. There's no confusion here.

Bracco went on to tell the court that he had no idea that I won an Emmy in 2011 for continuing coverage. He had no input on me not being selected for the Leadership Champion position. He described it as a corporate initiate that ultimately the department heads decided on. For me, that would have been Carrie Hofmann. The same was true for the decision not to hire me for the investigative reporter position that was filled by a former nurse. He all but exonerated himself of any of the decisions regarding the claims in my case, except the decision to promote Lindsay Shively.

At this point, Bracco had explained why a number of employee were not good fits and not renewed, including the biracial anchor who Lindsay Shively replaced. But when my attorney asked Bracco if there was any reason why I would not be a good fit for the investigative reporter position, he said no. I don't understand why, but him, sitting in his white male privilege, admitting there was no reason I was not given the promotion validated me in a sad and pathetic way. Here I am, a more than forty-year-old wife, mother, homeowner, and Emmy Award-winning journalist sitting in a federal courtroom for a discrimination and retaliation case, and somewhere in my warped psyche, I still felt good that Bracco validated me. Centering whiteness and aligning whiteness with rightness was clearly still pumping through my veins, even on this day. Why did it matter what this now retired white man said about me, especially considering that when he had the power to offer me an opportunity for growth he ignored me? But nonetheless, his words still meant something to me, which meant I still had a lot of work to do on myself, and my self-worth in the journey toward my racial identity and my own internalized racial oppression. I had a lot of work to do.

I first learned of the term IRO (internalized racial oppression) during the Kansas City mayor's community forums on race in 2018. The facilitator, Pakou Her, described IRO as a multigenerational socialization process that teaches people of color to believe, accept, and live out negative societal definitions of self and to fit into and live out inferior societal roles. When she explained that as I sat in the audience, it was like wheels in my head started turning. Immediately, I started mentally gnawing on the part where she said one believes "negative societal definitions of self," and we "live out inferior societal roles."

I kept reading and rereading the IRO definition over the coming days, and it dawned on me. The reason why it took me twelve years to finally file a grievance about being overlooked for positions and ultimately not even being able to get off the weekends was because I had somewhere along the line started to believe for myself what my white superiors saw in me. In my conscious mind, I wanted to grow into a weekend anchor position and mimic the fabulous career of Shaunya Chavis during my college years at WSB-TV. But in my subconscious mind, the fact that my white superiors didn't validate me in that position made me question my own talent, career, and self-worth. I accepted that if my bosses didn't see it in me, then maybe it's just not there.

As I sat in the courtroom feeling good about Bracco validating me, I knew that I still had a lot of work to do in valuing my authentic black self. It was painfully clear, through my reaction to his words, that I still believed that I was inferior to him, and I still wanted him to approve of me. How sad.

Before leaving the stand, Bracco admitted to the jurors that by the time he retired in 2017, he and Carrie Hofmann had put all white people in all of the primary news slots at KSHB-TV. Those prime time slots, included the morning show, the 6:00 p.m. newscast and the 10:00 p.m. newscast.

In my mind, hearing him say that was pretty damning, considering he admitted to nonrenewing, terminating, and demoting a number of minorities on staff. Unfortunately, I didn't believe Bracco's obvious bias in favor of whites resonated with the jurors as noticeably. I was concerned that my seven white jurors would see no problem with the white people working the preferred prime time positions, and the people of color working the weekends or wherever we were lucky enough to get a position.

Divide and Conquer—DelMeko Jordan

I only had three black people allowed to testify as witnesses for my side of the case. DelMeko Jordan was one of those people. He was a progressive young black man determined to make his mark. He earned a place on my witness list because he was the photographer I was working with, one of the two times an expletive made it on air in one of my stories. The first time, I finished editing a photographer's story for him and didn't notice that a man that was captured in video of people tailgating had an expletive on his shirt. At the time, I argued that I didn't shoot the video, nor was I expecting to edit it. But Carrie Hofmann, my news director, held me responsible for the error because she said I was the "final gatekeeper" for the package before it hit air. I accepted responsibility for the error because I was the person who sent it in to be aired.

Now fast-forward to the second time, an expletive made air in my story in August of 2017. DelMeko Jordan, a young black male photographer was editing his video and a technical glitch unblurred a screengrab he'd blurred. As a result, the bad words were clear for the viewers to see. He and I were doing a story about shoplifters, and the dayside executive producer sent us a website where thieves essentially bragged about their shoplifting hauls. And these sophisticated criminals used a lot of bad words to describe their stolen goods. DelMeko said he blurred the bad words before sending it in for air, but apparently, the edits he made to cover up the expletives disappeared. So when it aired in the six thirty newscast, it had a number of f-bombs. I didn't even know about the mistake until the next day because I left the live shot location, grabbed my things at the station, and went home. The next morning, Carrie Hofmann informed me of the mistake and sent me home. It was clear to me that I was not the final gatekeeper on this story, but nonetheless, I was being held responsible for the error. This, despite the fact that a second photographer, was sent to the live shot location to help DelMeko with the technical problems and the fact that DelMeko took full responsibility for the mistake. At the time, Carrie didn't tell me what my ultimate punishment would be. She simply informed me that the incident was being investigated, and she would let me know what they decided.

DelMeko called me on the day of my suspension. He was terrified that I was going to be fired for his mistake. To be honest, I was worried too. He and I had a transparent, eye-opening conversation about the training he was not receiving at KSHB-TV as an editor and part-time photographer. He shared with me that he desperately wanted to grow into a full-time photographer position but questioned if that opportunity would ever be available to him. I immediately questioned if he too, as a black man, would be dismissed and denied any opportunities. I was hopeful that his tenacity and youth would work in his favor, but I couldn't help but think of the other black male photographer who'd been on staff for more than fourteen years but still had not earned his way off weekends. I didn't tell him, but I doubted if anyone at KSHB-TV would ever see his potential or care about his hopes and plans for his own career.

Shortly thereafter, I was told that I would be suspended without pay for three days. I was pissed that I was the only person suspended for the on-air mistake, seeing as I didn't edit the story, and I wasn't the "final gatekeeper," but I was relieved that I had not been fired.

While on the stand, DelMeko recounted the mistake, took responsibility for it again, and proudly told the jurors about taking a new job at KMBC-9 news as a full-time nightside photographer. This job gave him exactly what he wanted, a chance to work and prove himself as a photographer and a competitive wage that allowed him to care for his family—an opportunity that was not available to him at KSHB-TV. In Carrie Hofmann's testimony, she described the same incident, and despite DelMeko taking responsibility, Hofmann said I blamed the photographer. Never mind the fact that he took responsibility for the error and informed her of the computer glitch. She was squarely focused on blaming me.

Sitting at the plaintiff's table, I was so proud of DelMeko, not for being willing to speak his truth in front of eight strangers but for not allowing KSHB-TV to have the final say on who he was or his career. I had so much admiration for this young twentysome-thing-year-old man for rejecting KSHB-TV's presumptions of him and pursuing an opportunity with a company that saw him as he saw himself—a full-time photographer who deserved to be fairly com-pensated for his talent.

I think DelMeko's honest testimony and clear disappointment in KSHB-TV's treatment of me and him resonated with the jurors. I truly thought the jurors believed that my suspension in this situ-ation was undeserved and retaliatory because Carrie Hofmann and KSHB-TV wanted to punish me for daring to accuse them of racial discrimination.

Next Up, News Director, Carrie Hofmann

Up next, my white female news director. She told me in April of 2015 that despite my more than twelve years of television news experience and my Emmy Award win for "Continuing Coverage," I was not a strong enough reporter to get off weekends. It was my pleasure to sit there and watch her flip her hair and bobblehead her way through the questions.

My attorney immediately started having her validate documents. From the multiple e-mails I'd sent her about scheduling to my complaints about bullying, preferential treatment, and discrimination, Carrie told the jurors that corporate leadership had kept her abreast of my internal complaints launched via corporate HR in Cincinnati. But when it was time for her to validate those e-mails, there was an objection by the defense counsel that lead to a break.

The problem behind the scenes and out of the hearing of the jurors was that part of the defense's case included, saying I hadn't complained about differential treatment until after my May 26, 2015, suspension for the tone of my voice. My attorney was attempting to get in documents through Carrie Hofmann that proved that both she and corporate HR had knowledge of my discrimination concerns before my suspension. At one point, my attorney, Dennis Egan, told the judge, "My view is that there's some games being played by the defendant in keeping us from getting at the truth. This is a true fact."

The document in question was generated by a corporate HR lady and produced by the defendant about a conversation I had with HR about the differential treatment I was experiencing and witnessing at work. The defense attorney was desperately trying to block it from being admitted into evidence.

Despite saying that corporate would keep her abreast of any discrimination complaints, Carrie testified she had never seen the document. My attorney continued by reading the document line by line, highlighting the system failure that would result in my launching a complaint of this magnitude and corporate allegedly not informing the current news director.

My attorney asked, "Did you know that Lisa Benson told Julie Moorehouse that she feels as though she is not getting opportunities at KSHB and that she has not been getting feedback about the reasons why in the past?"

Carrie answered, "I don't know what Lisa told Julie Moorehouse."

My attorney also asked Carrie if she knew about the schedule manipulations that I believed station leadership enacted to get people to quit. He went on to name a few people of color who'd been demoted from their positions and ultimately quit and got out of the business.

Carrie responded no.

My attorney also brought up the hiring preferences I noted in the 2015 conversation with corporate HR. At the time, it was painfully clear that the new GM had an affinity for young white women.

"Did you know she told Julie Moorehouse, quote, 'Bracco likes pretty white young girls. Blondes with a big chest. They have not hired anyone on air over thirty since Bracco started. It's clear what he is going for. As a black female in my late thirties, I know I'll never fit what Bracco wants.'"

Carrie continued to answer "no" as my attorney introduced the contents of the document into evidence without introducing the exhibit. I was so proud of my attorney for forcing the defense counsel to accept its own document despite their efforts to create a false story line.

The next document outlined the May 21, 2015, discussion with Melissa Greenstein that resulted in me being suspended for the tone of my voice. Carrie described what I considered a discussion over the use of file video as a verbal attack.

"Lisa yelled at her in the newsroom when they were having a feedback session," Carrie told the jurors.

Here we go. My white female news director was right on script, painting me as the aggressive angry black woman who disrespected authority and yelled at her bosses. Wow.

My attorney had her go over the mundane contents of the e-mail, including the location of the flooding story, the question over the need for file video, and my explanation as to why I used new video. Carrie explained the difference in the video I was using, which was ground video shot the day of versus the older aerial video that was shot over the weekend. In her conversations about the video and admitting I put the video in as Greenstein hadrequested, it was almost awkward when she talked about why I was suspended.

My attorney introduced my suspension letter, which was my very first reprimand during my entire career at KSHB-TV. In the letter, which would serve as my first and final warning, Carrie wrote, "Your job is in jeopardy."

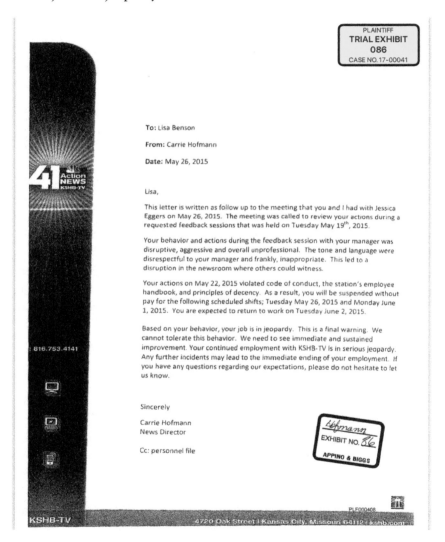

To: Lisa Benson

From: Carrie Hofmann

Date: May 26, 2015

Lisa,

This letter is written as follow up to the meeting that you and I had with Jessica Eggers on May 26, 2015. The meeting was called to review your actions during a requested feedback sessions that was held on Tuesday May 19th, 2015.

Your behavior and actions during the feedback session with your manager was disruptive, aggressive and overall unprofessional. The tone and language were disrespectful to your manager and frankly, inappropriate. This led to a disruption in the newsroom where others could witness.

Your actions on May 22, 2015 violated code of conduct, the station's employee handbook, and principles of decency. As a result, you will be suspended without pay for the following scheduled shifts; Tuesday May 26, 2015 and Monday June 1, 2015. You are expected to return to work on Tuesday June 2, 2015.

Based on your behavior, your job is in jeopardy. This is a final warning. We cannot tolerate this behavior. We need to see immediate and sustained improvement. Your continued employment with KSHB-TV is in serious jeopardy. Any further incidents may lead to the immediate ending of your employment. If you have any questions regarding our expectations, please do not hesitate to let us know.

Sincerely

Carrie Hofmann
News Director

Cc: personnel file

EXHIBIT NO. 86
APPINO & BIGGS

PLF000408

816.753.4141

KSHB-TV   4720 Oak Street | Kansas City, Missouri 64112 | kshb.com

This suspension letter was especially frightening to me because it was my first time ever being disciplined at KSHB-TV, and I didn't understand why the normal progressive discipline options didn't apply to me. Why didn't I get a written warning? I didn't have a history of yelling at my bosses. Why wasn't I even included in the investigation? Despite my questions, concerns, and confusion at the time, I had no power to change anything. My white female supervisor was offended by my tone. My white female boss believed I had been offensive, and the white female human resources director at the time believed everything they said without so much as a conversation with me. Their white solidarity was strong, and I, as a black woman, had no voice nor power against them.

I knew at that moment that I did not have a voice, and my concerns would not be addressed at KSHB-TV if I wasn't willing to report this unfair, atrocious treatment to someone who could hold them accountable. I had already considered hiring an attorney and filing an EEOC. But now I knew I had to do it, not only for myself but for the countless other people of color who had and continued to be silenced and redefined by this company. Station leadership was fully aligned in their effort to protect their white advantages and keep others in their place.

I'll never forget the drive to the EEOC office. It took me across the state line to Kansas City, Kansas. I sat there talking to a man and filling out paperwork. It felt a bit redundant, but I was willing to fill out as much paperwork needed to start my official complaint against my employer. The EEOC investigator asked me how long the discrimination had been going on. I sat there, thinking back to the time when I was sent to the home of a known KKK member alone for a story. I also thought about the numerous times I applied for advancement at KSHB-TV, including the weekend anchor position that went to a white female colleague who didn't even apply for it. I remembered leaving the EEOC office and stopping at the Popham Law Firm and talking to the paralegal. When I stopped, I was looking for Dennis Egan. I had already done some research on the Christine Craft case, a white woman who sued KMBC in 1983 for discrimination, and three other women who sued KMBC for age and sex discrimination in 2008. Dennis Egan represented the women in both cases. I knew walking into his downtown office that if anyone had a chance of winning a discrimination lawsuit against a media giant like E. W. Scripps, it was Egan, a confident tall, slender white man. After all, you have to fight fire with fire. If I had any hopes of convincing a jury of my truth, I thought I needed a white man to fight for me.

Carrie's testimony continued along with a host of e-mails showing that I was suspended for not supervising a photographer's work when it is impossible to always be in a position to supervise. There were countless times when a photographer was working on my story, and I was sent out to breaking news with another photographer. In those situations, like every day, a photographer has to be responsible for his own work. But nonetheless, Carrie told the jurors that reporters and photographers were a team, and I should have watched the story before it aired. I think between DelMeko's testimony and Carrie's blaming, the jurors could clearly see that mandated supervising of a photographer's story was reserved for me, the one person suing the station for discrimination.

The jurors also heard how I was excluded from beat days. Beat days are days that reporters get to dig up exclusive stories, do research, connect with sources, and work without being responsible for content in the newscast. My attorney showed how, despite my requests, I was denied beat days when my white coworkers were given plenty. My attorney read an e-mail that pretty much surmised how I felt at the time with the microaggressions that made a huge impact on my day-to-day dealings in the newsroom. I wrote in an e-mail to HR, "I know Carrie has full power to treat her employees as she sees fit, which includes preferred schedules, shifts and the allotment of beat days, but this is clearly another example of how preferred employees are given consideration and advantages that help them perform better. The same is not true for me in the newsroom."

I believe after the e-mail, I was assigned more beat days, but this is another example of the constant fighting I had to do in this newsroom for equality now that I dared to file a grievance, demanding that this company do better.

Then Carrie had to admit that after my 2015 suspension for the tone of my voice, I was banned from being able to fill in on the anchor desk. At the time, they said I wasn't a strong enough fill-in anchor anymore. I needed to improve to be considered for fill-in work. This, after years of filling in on the anchor desk. In my mind, this was further proof of retaliation. Miraculously, they reinstated my ability to fill in 2017 for the Thanksgiving weekend. This fill-in anchoring opportunity became available as we were approaching my April 2018 trial date. To me, it was obvious they wanted to get me back on the fill-in anchoring roster so that it didn't look like me being yanked from it was further punishment for the tone of my voice in 2015 or better yet, retaliation for filing a lawsuit.

There were other e-mails that I'd written to HR that my attorney tried to get into evidence but the judge would not allow. The defense counsel also continued its objection to talking to other black employees about their experiences at KSHB-TV, saying their experiences were not similarly situated, in particular, DelMeko Jordan. His testimony was limited to my three-day suspension, not how he too felt excluded from growth opportunities that were available to white photographers.

My attorney tried to get into an on-air mistake that resulted in an August 2017 lawsuit being filed against the station. A Missouri couple said they were allegedly negatively depicted in a report about a man charged with tricking women into having sex while being filmed. File video of the couple was used and the graphic read, "Man Charged with Tricking Women into On-Camera Sex." The couple was outraged, and they filed a lawsuit, but no one involved in writing, editing, or reporting that story lost their job despite the fact that someone's error lead to a lawsuit. Unfortunately, the judge did not see a correlation between my situation and this situation. My attorney also tried to get in an e-mail from a viewer who was complaining about KSHB-TV's racist coverage of a local news event. Hofmann responded saying she didn't believe the coverage was racist and thanked the viewer for her e-mail. My attorney's point was to show that Hofmann, in the ordinary course of business, had the sole discretion to define racism at KSHB-TV, as a middle-aged white woman running a news organization in Kansas City, and how her opinion dictated coverage despite how viewers felt. Unfortunately, the judge decided the viewer's e-mail was irrelevant. So the jurors never heard or saw several pieces of evidence that my attorney and I thought were clear cases of bias and differential treatment.

Listening to Carrie Hofmann's testimony, it was hard to believe that she was trying to convince the jurors that she didn't know that I had race-based complaints. Despite our e-mails and conversations, she told the jurors, "I didn't not know Lisa had any issue with race until the EEOC."

In my opinion, Hofmann was lying. Unfortunately, the jurors did not get to consider all the race-based issues or complaints I'd had at the station since I started working. Based on the rules of engagement in federal court, only three promotion opportunities were in play for my case because of the time that had passed. Essentially, some of my experiences at KSHB-TV were too old to bring up in court. Nonetheless, Carrie went on to tell the jurors that my discrimination concerns conveyed to local HR and corporate HR were not conveyed to her, ever. However, she agreed that she did consult the same local HR lady to decide on my 2015 punishment for the tone of my voice. An investigation and suspension they both seemingly agreed did not need my input.

The juror question-and-answer part was very interesting, following Carrie's testimony. A number of the juror questions were omitted, but the first question for Hofmann was, "What kind of training did you receive when you got the news director position in regards to diversity in the workplace and equal opportunity?"

I thought to myself, "Great question, jurors!"

She replied, "So I get lots of training." She went onto explain how she was taught employment law, libel laws, code of conduct, and the rules of slander in TV news, but she didn't even use the word diversity in her answer. In my mind, it was painfully clear that diversity is not a priority for this company or this news director. I don't know if the jurors caught that, but I did.

When Carrie was called back on the stand by the defense counsel, our committed jurors came with another great question. It was about the conversation Carrie overheard in the bathroom between Christa Dubill and I about a story I was working on. The question asked, "Why did you talk to Christa Dubill instead of Lisa Benson who was having issues with management?"

Her answer, which I should have predicted was, "Honestly, I was afraid of approaching Lisa for fear of her having a negative reaction or considering it retaliation."

It was clear to me throughout Carrie's testimony that she was afraid of me. How can anyone be expected to value, promote, or even have meaningful interactions with someone whom they're genuinely afraid of? It doesn't happen. She is case in point of why white people need to be exposed to people of color in their personal lives so they don't have to be afraid when they're forced to work beside them.

Next Up, Me!

During trial preparations, my attorney told me that I wouldn't take the stand until Friday. Thanks to time limits and a lot of sidebar conversations at the bench, I took the stand earlier than expected. My husband, despite being on our witness list, wasn't called at all because my attorney was running out of time.

I'm almost embarrassed to admit that I went through four outfits trying to decide what I was going to wear on my first day on the stand. I landed on a dress with a flash of color, covered by a tailored black jacket. I wanted the jurors to see me as the anchor I never was at KSHB-TV while reaffirming my professionalism.

After raising my right hand to be sworn in, my attorney had me talk to the jurors about my professional history and background. Looking at the jurors, I told them about my upbringing in Moberly, Missouri, and my family's subsequent move to St. Louis, Missouri, when I was around twelve or thirteen. I told them of my numerous internships, including one at CNN as I pursued my mass media arts degree at Clark Atlanta University.

The more he asked these foundation setting questions, the more at ease I felt on the stand. Throughout the trial, I had friends and community members who would sit in the courtroom. As I answered my attorney's questions, I would look out at my friend, Lora McDonald and Heather Staggers, to gauge their reactions.

Their gentle smiles and nods gave me the assurance and confidence that I was being received well by the jurors.

Through my two and a half days of testimony, both of my sisters attended the proceedings. Thank God they were not on the witness list, like my husband and a few other former coworkers who wanted to watch the show. Both of my sisters would smile or silently mouth the word "slow" so that I would know that I was talking too fast. I've always been a fast-talker, and my attorney reminded me numerous times to take my time so the jurors could understand me and connect with me through my story.

I told the jurors about the TV jobs I held at KQTV in St. Joseph, Missouri, and WAND-TV in Decatur, Illinois. In both positions, I was expected to edit my own work. At KQTV, I was a one-man band reporter, who set up, wrote, shoot, edited, and presented my own stories every day. At that station, after about a year and a half, I was promoted to the weekend anchor position.

My attorney went on to introduce my contracts at KSHB-TV into evidence after showcasing my professional journey to Kansas City. As I sat there looking at a copy of my contract, I was almost embarrassed at how little money I made. In my first contract in 2004 with KSHB-TV, I made $40,000.00 for the first year and $41,200.00 for the second year of my contract.

In my 2017 contract, I made $25.75 an hour, which was $53,560.00 a year, that meant after being with the company for thirteen years, I had made just over $13,000.00 dollars a year in a pay jump. Talk about internalized racial oppression. I clearly thought very little of myself to show up to work each day for more than a decade and become an Emmy Award-winning journalist, without any expectation of a competitive salary. I knew that the white reporters being hired were making more than me. But for some reason, I wasn't furious. I should have been.

My attorney moved from my low-earning contracts to the story that lead to me and the station's investigative reporter at that time getting our first regional Emmys in 2011.

I told the court that a young black man who'd spent years in prison contacted me about recovering his mother's ashes. She died while he was in prison. Not only was he not able to attend the funeral, but after being released, he learned that no one ever retrieved her ashes from the funeral home due to unpaid cremation expenses. After doing the heart-wrenching story with him about his loss, the man who now owned the property of the abandoned funeral home reached out to me. He told me he not only owned the property but would allow us to access it to see if the young man could find his mother's ashes. Within a week, I was shooting the story alone at the vacant funeral home with the man and the owner of the property. My MMJ kit did not have a light, so I called in a favor to a photographer friend. I asked him to come to the property to shoot in the dark basement in hopes of finding this man's ashes. My photographer friend, Fernando Ochoa, was more than willing to oblige. Fernando's camera was rolling as we entered the dark dusty basement of this abandoned funeral home and saw hundreds of standing rectangular boxes. Each black box had a white label and a name on it. Immediately, we realized there were cremated remains in the boxes. The man started looking for his mother's name. Within minutes, he found it. He found his mother's name, and we caught this tearful, sad, and eerie moment on camera. I felt victorious for helping find this man's mother followed by great sadness that she and the hundreds of other people in this dark basement had been forgotten and left behind.

We returned to the station and did a great emotional follow-up to this man's story. The next day, the news director at the time and the supervisor of the investigative unit told me that I did a great job on the story and informed me that they were turning the story over to Ryan Kath. They said Ryan, as an investigator, would have more time to devote to the story and reuniting more abandoned ashes with living relatives. Despite him being hired as a general assignment reporter, just like me, Ryan had been promoted to the station's investigative reporter position.

At the time, I was so grateful that they saw value in a story that I saw value in. I didn't have enough sense to realize that they were taking my story and giving it to Ryan Kath to help promote and validate him as an investigative reporter—a position that garnered more money and prestige within the industry. I turned all my information and contacts over to Ryan. He went on to do more follow-up stories about reuniting people with the unclaimed ashes of their dead loved ones.

In 2011, the station submitted the stories to the 2011 Mid-America NATAS Emmy Awards for Continuing Coverage, and the stories were nominated. At the time, I had no expectation of winning. I knew Ryan had been nominated before, but winning was clearly a more difficult feat. The NATAS regional Emmy pitted journalists across the region against one another. After all, this was a story station management had no interest in, and I had never even been to an Emmy gala before. Surely, there were far better reporters and investigators out there. Nonetheless, I borrowed a dress from one of my closest friends, Katrina McCann, who also styled me for the event, and my husband drove me to St. Louis. My sister Norma, always the supportive big sister, bought a ticket and donned a pretty dress for the event.

I remember having no concern about possibly winning. In fact, I told the jurors, "I didn't expect to win. This was the first time they'd submitted any of my work. This was the first time I had a conversation about Emmys. In fact, I had to join the organization just so my work could be submitted because I wasn't even a member."

I sat there in my fancy dress, sitting at this fancy round table next to my husband and sister as my category and story came up. I was nothing short of shocked when the announcer said for Continuing Coverage, "Ashes to Ashes KSHB-TV," followed by my name, that of the photographer, Fernando Ochoa and Ryan Kath.

I remembered getting on the stage, and despite it being my story, slinking back to allow Ryan Kath to take center stage and speak. He accepted the award. I looked at him, nodded, and smiled, just like a good nigger would. The irony of this "white privilege" moment in 2011 is not lost on me in 2019. A black woman finds the story, pursues the story, gets the story, convinces a Latino man to volunteer to work the story only for it to be given to a white man so he can use it to catapult his career and accept the glory. Wow. It's crazy even writing this book now how white-centered and protective of white people I was. How I too believed they deserved the accolades, the best of everything, and I was just lucky to have a job and be among them. Even if it was my work who got us there. Damn, I can't help but wonder what was so wrong with me that I thought so little of myself. But this journey through knowledge and understanding after my termination has helped me understand that I, like so many others, was socialized to believe that whiteness was the norm and the standard by which we all should be measured. Sad.

In subsequent years, I would do a number of stories that I would suggest for an Emmy submission, including a story about a Kansas City real estate company that was ultimately sued by the Missouri Attorney General's office for tricking low-income residents out of their money under the illusion of investing toward homeownership. They told people they would essentially be renting to own their own homes if they were willing to make the payments and put in sweat equity to transform these vacant houses into livable homes. My story was instrumental in uncovering the deception and put the ring leader of the fraud behind bars. I asked station leadership if they would submit my work for a Mid-America Emmy. They said no. At the time, I didn't have the expendable personal income myself to invest money in hopes of getting another Emmy. But from the standpoint of KSHB-TV station management, it was crystal clear to me that without a white person to support, my work would not be celebrated at KSHB-TV. They had no reason to validate me or my work. After all, they knew even back then that there would be no opportunities for growth for me, so any more Emmys would only make proving my inconsistency and lack of talent as a reporter harder for them.

My attorney and I continued our back-and-forth question and answer session for the remainder of the day minus breaks and a lot of conversations at the bench. I explained to the jurors how I applied for the jobs that we're being considered in the trial, which included a 2013 weekend anchor position that was awarded to Lindsay Shively. The defense counsel would later argue that I did not complete my online application for the process, therefore, essentially nullifying my interest and application. This despite the fact that Lindsay admitted to never filling out an application or formerly applying for any of the promotions she got at KSHB-TV. It was painfully clear that I was expected to play by a different set of rules while my white coworkers were being seamlessly promoted into better, higher-paying positions.

I also told the jurors about me agreeing to switch shifts with a white female reporter named Beth Vaughn in 2012 in hopes of getting more opportunities to fill in on the anchor desk. My news director, at the time, told me the shift change would put me in a better position to fill-in anchor. I foolishly believed her. Within the year, Beth Vaughn was promoted to a Scripps station in Indianapolis as the morning anchor, a position she held until January of 2018. In January of 2018, I was still working weekends at KSHB-TV. And now, according to my news director, Carrie Hofmann, unqualified to return to the Monday through Friday dayside shift I once held. We told the jurors about other positions within the company I applied for that I was never even interviewed for, including an anchor/reporter position at the Scripps station in Denver, Colorado. At the time, I thought KSHB-TV selfishly wanted to keep me for themselves at the station because I didn't question my talent level. I was a good reporter and a solid anchor. Now it's clear that in the eyes of leadership, my black skin was best suited for the weekends at KSHB-TV so they could promote deserving white people into those coveted, higher-paying positions throughout the company.

My attorney showed how after his hiring in 2013, Brian Bracco clearly had little interest in the women of color anchors. He refused to offer another contract to one biracial anchor and demoted an Asian woman. All these moves in his commitment to promote Lindsay Shively, a white woman into a Monday through Friday morning anchor position.

We were able to successfully show the jury how my performance evaluations up through 2014 were favorable. They weren't perfect, but I met expectations, and there was no reason that I shouldn't have been give at least one opportunity for growth. It wasn't until 2015 when I started questioning the disparate treatment that I was suddenly suspended for the tone of my voice and started performing below expectations. I explained to the jurors that I applied for the investigative reporter position in 2015, and Carrie Hofmann boldly told me that I was not qualified for the position because I didn't have data mining experience in an investigative unit. I feared that some of the TV jargon was being lost on the jurors, so I tried to explain what an investigative unit was versus what a general assignment reporter did. Essentially, an investigator works on longer stories that require more research and time. And investigators are given that time to dig into their stories. In contrast, general assignment reporters dig for information, but their stories have to be finished each day, making it impossible for a real deep dive for information and proof that should be typical of an investigative story. I went on to explain to the jurors, "I think all reporters data mine. Data is information. Mining is digging. As reporters, you're always digging for information, that's the crux of what we do."

I went on to tell the jurors that I volunteered to work in the investigative position for Carrie as she continued to look for an experienced candidate. Carrie turned down my offer. At the time, I didn't fully understand why, but overtime, it became clear that she could not afford for me to succeed because then they would again have to justify the lack of promotion opportunities available to me. It's easier for leadership to say I'm not qualified for opportunities that are never presented to me than to await my failure because they knew after years of begging for an opportunity for growth, I would not have allowed myself to fail. I would have delivered content four days out of the five-day workweek as I had promised—a commitment to quality and quantity that no other investigator had ever attempted to produce. Some of our previous investigators would go an entire week without putting a single story on air. But had they allowed me to succeeded, they would have had no excuse to keep me in my lower-paying weekend shift. Instead, Carrie refused my offer and went on to hire Jessica McMaster, who had less reporting experience and had never worked in an investigative unit. And prior to trial, it had never really dawned on me, but all the investigators at KSHB-TV since I was hired were white people. In almost fifteen years, not one person of color had earned their way to the coveted position. I guess I was a bit foolish to think that somehow, I was going to bust through that black ceiling. I call it a "black ceiling" because with a glass ceiling, you can at least see the floors you'll never ascend to. A black ceiling includes the smoke and mirrors of denied opportunities and denied knowledge of the opportunities. In many of the promotions that were happening around me in my more than fourteen years at KSHB-TV, I didn't even know the positions were open until they sent out an e-mail, informing everyone that the position had been filled. In all those cases, the person who got the promotion was white. Ironically, the same was true for the employees the company invested in to attend IRE (investigative, reporters, and editors) conferences. During my time at KSHB-TV, they did not send one person of color to the IRE professional development conference. I told the jurors about my requests to attend the annual training and the station's refusal to invest in me or my career goals.

At this point, I'd been on the witness stand for a while, and I kept forgetting to look at the jurors when answering my attorney's questions. In the few times I remembered to look over, I would catch a brief smile from an older white woman, which was encouraging. I also remember the forty-something white woman on the second row who never smiled. I couldn't tell if she lacked interest in the trial altogether or just in me and my story. Nonetheless, Dennis' questions kept coming, and I kept answering them. I answered questions about the ongoing reporter feedback I was receiving under a previous manager and how that precluded Carrie's 2015 revelation that I was all of a sudden an inconsistent, unbalanced reporter with performance issues. And according to Carrie, the only reason I wasn't aware of my inadequacies as a reporter is because I had not received adequate feedback from management. The e-mails, introduced into court, further proved that she knew I had problems with the way I was being treated under her leadership. This e-mail followed my failed attempt to get off weekends.

Benson, Lisa

From:	Benson, Lisa
Sent:	Monday, April 27, 2015 11:21 PM
To:	Hofmann, Carrie; Greenstein, Melissa; Eggers, Jessica
Cc:	Bracco, Brian; Moorehouse, Julie
Subject:	Follow-up meeting

Hi,

I am deeply saddened by the derogatory remarks made today during the meeting about my schedule. For the first time during my employment with KSHB-TV, I was informed that:

"I have performance issues"

"I am inconsistent"

"It's best for the station if I stay on weekends"

"You're not strong enough to work the <u>Monday through Friday</u> shift"

"Your stories are unbalanced"

"I don't think you have enough contacts"

After reviewing my 2014 annual review, none of the above mentioned problems were noted.

In fact, my manager confirmed that I am "fully meeting the expectations of my position" in *all* categories including core competencies, communication, creativity, news gathering and storytelling.

I was even applauded for my passion in the newsroom.

I have asked for feedback, training and the opportunity to grow with E.W. Scripps countless times during my 11 year tenure.
The disparity between the insults hurled at me today and what is on my review highlights the bullying that remains a problem among newsroom leadership.

The leaders in this newsroom have consistently shown preferential treatment to some employees while suppressing others.

I have reservations about meeting again tomorrow, but remain hopeful that there will be a resolution.

Sincerely,

Greenstein
EXHIBIT NO. 21
APPINO & BIGGS

PLF000622

1

This conversation and exchange happened about a month before I was suspended for the tone of my voice. I worried that hearing this information again, after hearing it during Carrie's testimony, was becoming redundant for the jurors. But I had to remember that now I had the chance to tell my story, my truth, so I kept reminding myself to slow down while speaking so the jurors could make the connection between my scathing evaluation when seeking to get off weekends, the subsequent suspension for the tone of my voice, and the now recurring performance issues—issues that were created to prove that I am unqualified to get off weekends. I, as a black woman at KSHB-TV, am only good enough to work in support roles to my white counterparts who deserve Monday through Friday shifts and weekends off with their family. This disparate treatment was devastatingly clear to me, but I questioned if it was resonating with my jury of seven white people and one Indian man. I was especially concerned about the four white women who would ultimately decide my fate.

The questions and answers soon took us to Mosby, Missouri, for a flooding story that would ultimately lead to me being suspended for the tone of my voice. My attorney had me set the scene in this small Missouri town that was experiencing flooding. I went on to explain why I decided to use my fresh day of video in my short on-air stories versus using the older file video from the weekend. Again, I thought some of the TV jargon was boring to the jurors, but I thought my explanation would help the jurors see just how insignificant this editorial decision was in the field. The station had the file video that they could have used in the tease video and the opening video. This issue was not an issue outside of station management, trying to find fault with me. Truly, my decision not to use file video was my resolve to write to video and move the story forward for the viewer. But when Melissa Greenstein instructed us to put it in, my photographer did just that. This was clearly blown into an angry-black-girl moment to create an opportunity to punish me as they doubled down on the efforts to fault find and prove that I was unworthy of weekends off or any level of opportunity within the company.

Before digging deep into the nuances of the conversation and the suspension, we ended the day's testimony because it was 5:00 p.m. So I stepped off the witness stand, knowing full well that I would be first up the next morning to continue trying to convince the jury that I wasn't whom the defense counsel was painting me out to be.

As I walked back to my table and ultimately the conference room reserved for my legal team, I couldn't help but look at the two tables of the attorneys that were sitting on the defense side and think, finally, they have to listen to my voice. For years at KSHB-TV, I wanted to be seen, and I wanted to be heard; and in a subtle and passive way, the company told me that I had little value, and my voice didn't count. And now they are paying hundreds of thousands of dollars to their legal team to sit and not only listen to me but to dissect what I am saying. In that, I had to trust that some accountability structures would be implemented. Because truth be told, if they were not going to give me a chance to grow with the company, they could have kindly not renewed my contract year after year, which is something they had done to other reporters in the past.

The trial was nerve-wracking, but at that point, despite the e-mails and offers to settle the case, I knew I had to finish. If not for me but for every person of color who comes behind me who wants to be seen and heard.

The jurors left the courtroom, but the attorneys on both sides had a lot to talk to the judge about following my testimony. A big focus of the conversations was Facebook posts. As part of the discovery portion of the trial, I had to turn over a download of all my social media pages. I mean everything. My personal and professional Facebook pages, my Twitter page, my Instagram page, even my Poshmark page I used to buy used fancy clothes and shoes. With all that personal information, the defense team found a post I shared on my personal page in 2018 of someone comparing a photograph of sleeveless Michelle Obama that was deemed inappropriate by someone to a nude photograph of Melania Trump that was referred to as art by those very same groups. I didn't comment on the post. I shared it. The defense was fighting to get the controversial Facebook share to the jurors under the rule of "after acquired evidence." After acquired evidence in employment law is essentially facts the employer learns after firing an employee, for which the employer would have fired the employee anyway.

In response, my attorney argued that because both Christa and Jessica violated the social media policy but were not fired when their Facebook foul-ups were discovered, it was inadmissible. Christa was promoting products on her page, but Jessica clearly commented on politically charged views about President Trump that didn't warrant punishment by the station. Using her Facebook pseudonym Jessica Lynn, Jessica commented on a post of President Trump picture posted to a tree with the words, "Fugly Slut" on it. The Facebook post was shared on one of Jessica's friend's page. She liked it and commented on it, which was a violation of the station's social media guidelines.

Jessica's "Fugly Slut" Trial Exhibit 286

Instead of punishing Jessica McMaster for endorsing a negative depiction of the sitting president, according to the station's social media guidelines, KSHB-TV management offered her another contract with a significant pay raise.

Listening to the arguments on the defense's side, it was unbelievable to me how even in court, they were trying to hold me to a standard that they refused to expect of my white female counterparts. Did they not see that they were arguing that I should have been fired for sharing a post when they refused to hold their two still gainfully employed white employees accountable for their posts, even now? The white privilege and protection was painfully clear to me, but I prayed that my white female judge could at least see the contradiction and double standards, if not the obvious privilege of being white while working for KSHB-TV.

After listening to the bantering of the attorneys, I walked into the galley and motioned for my friend Lora McDonald to come to our little conference room. I was so encouraged when she told me I was doing well. She gave me her read on the jurors as I was speaking. She was confident that the male jurors were engaged in my story, but she too had concerns about the two white women who appeared to be in their forties. Her energy and optimism helped fuel me for the next day, and the plaintiff walk in the hallway. Every day the crowd of KSHB-TV and E. W. Scripps people swelled in the hallway because potential witnesses could not sit in the courtroom. So every evening, I would put on my coat, grab my things, throw my shoulders back to walk past my former bosses and coworkers. Accompanied by my legal team, we got on the elevator and went straight to the law office to debrief and prepare for the next day. I was exhausted but still motivated get back on the stand for day two.

Day Two of Testimony

I took the stand for the second day in my trial on February 1, 2019. It was crazy how much I debated what to wear. I generally gravitate to patterns, but I felt a solid color would pair best with the jurors. I landed on a solid burnt-orange dress with a black jacket.

Before getting back on the stand, my attorney called an income tax expert to the stand and a human resources business partner who no longer worked for the company. The middle-aged black woman, whom the company designated as their corporate HR representative, clearly did not want to be there. Despite a few questions from my attorney, she refused to talk about her reason for leaving the company or where she was currently working. It did seem like E. W. Scripps just wanted to put a black woman on the stand against me, seeing as she admitted to never talking to me or investigating any of the discrimination complaints I made against the company. The most significant part of her testimony, in my view, was when she had to admit that the company had no guidelines in the company handbook about the timely filing of tax returns. The income tax guy talked about the confidentiality of tax returns and how outside of the lawsuit, they would not have known that my husband had been late filing our returns. My attorney had to address this because my late filing of tax returns was also put on my termination letter as a reason for nonrenewal. My attorney made a point to ask my former coworkers if timely filing of tax returns was part of their job description. You could tell by their responses that they were even confused as to how tax returns had anything to do with my job or my termination.

After a brief recess, I was back on the stand, following the former human resources business partner. My attorney started with introducing a June 13, 2013, e-mail, where I was thanking news director, Carrie Hofmann, for allowing me to do a read through in my quest for an anchoring opportunity at the station. This e-mail would have been sent shortly after I'd returned from maternity leave after having my first son. This was just a few months after Carrie Hofmann had been hired. Before my attorney could introduce another document, the defense attorney objected. During the bench conversation, the attorney accused me of scripting e-mails and sending them to my attorney for approval while still employed and looking for growth opportunities at KSHB-TV. I was so insulted that they seriously thought that as a college-educated journalist, I did not have the knowledge base to craft an e-mail to my boss without my lawyer's approval. Some of the e-mails were dated before I'd even hired an attorney. After a few more rounds of these demeaning allegations, my attorney set him straight. He had not drafted or approved any of my e-mails. My attorney introduced e-mail after e-mail over the course of years where I was clearly petitioning for growth opportunities. Sitting there, it was embarrassing how many times I had applied for jobs that would never be available to me. At the time, I didn't realize how pathetic I looked, but going over these e-mails one by one, it was clear that I should have either given up or started fighting years prior to the 2016 filing of my lawsuit.

From the denied anchor opportunities, my attorney transitioned into me applying for the investigative reporter position in 2015. I told the jurors that I had already been validated as a strong reporter at KSHB-TV, so I thought growing into an investigative role would be a natural growth step for someone that they clearly did not see as an anchor.

I told the jurors that after years of unsuccessfully applying for anchor positions, an e-mail I drafted to Carrie in hopes of getting the investigative position was my surrender to the reality of my career limitations at KSHB-TV. I started crying as I told the courts, "It was my concession. You clearly don't see me as an anchor, so let me grow into this investigative role so I can continue to shine as an investigative reporter." This testimony was emotionally draining for me because I was clearly looking for my supervisors to validate me and my work and despite their unwillingness to do that. I continued to beg for their acceptance. Sitting on the stand, I didn't understand why, at the time, I didn't see it. But now, thanks to my study of diversity, inclusion, and anti-racism, it was clear to me why I, as a black woman, needed my white superiors to validate me. And to be honest, it wasn't just for monetary gain. The truth is, I felt more acceptable if white people accepted me. And this lack of opportunity was pure rejection. If it were just about money, I would have quit or looked for another job. The truth is, I wanted the white people I valued to value me.

After composing myself, I told the jurors how my April 2015 attempt at a promotion or a schedule change resulted in Carrie Hofmann telling me I was an inconsistent, incompetent reporter with performance issues. This was devastating for me because I had already conceded that I would never be an anchor for KSHB-TV, and now after eleven years, I'm not even a good reporter. At this point in my career, I felt backed against a wall. It was painfully clear that I would never grow. In 2015, I had one kid, and my husband and I were trying for number two. I couldn't quit, and I knew I would never be given the opportunity to grow in any capacity. So I had no choice but to fight.

My attorney went back over the file video for the flooding story that lead to my two-day suspension—a story the jurors had heard. At that point, I was pretty confident that the jurors could see the inconsistencies in my treatment. I told the jurors that I had such great video on the ground from the day of and that I did not need to use the old file video. But I did put it in after receiving a call from the executive producer at the time, Melissa Greenstein, asking me to put it in. I asked my photographer to put the video in, and he did. For us, it was not a big deal. At the time, we were navigating flooded roads while trying to follow the governor and make air on time. I felt the same way a few days later discussing the story with Melissa. Instead of accepting my journalistic decision to not use file video and acknowledging the fact that I respected her position in doing what I was instructed to do when I added the video, Melissa turned that conversation into her opportunity to be a white damsel in distress. And I was her assailant.

During the feedback session, Melissa told me that as a veteran journalist, I should have known to use file video. I believe, at that point, she expected her black female subordinate to lower her head in shame and apologize for daring to have an opposing viewpoint. Instead, I told her that as a veteran journalist, I knew it was my job to move the story forward and give the viewer fresh video and stories about what was going on now in Mosby, Missouri. She interrupted me, saying, "You're not listening to me."

I told the jurors, "It felt like another fault-finding mission to where no matter what I said, she was going to find fault in me. And so when I defended my reasoning for not using file video, instead of her understanding, she just got mad at me. She's the one who got up and walked away."

After she grabbed her purse and jacket and headed for the door, I got up, walked back to my desk, and finished working my shift that ended at 7:30 p.m.

In my opinion, the conversation was not combative or disrespectful. We simply had a difference of journalistic opinions. Honestly, I was surprised when I got an e-mail from her, and I was subsequently suspended for the tone of my voice.

In hindsight, this was her effort at control and intimidation. It had become clear to me that in our feedback session, I did not exude enough fear; therefore, she called upon her white privilege and solidarity to ensure my punishment. I was punished for answering the questions posed to me in a manner that did not exude the lowliness, shame, and humility that is befitted a black subordinate. The suspension letter, which was the first discipline issue in my personnel file in my entire career at KSHB-TV, read that this was my "first and final" warning.

In the meeting where I was being informed of my two-day suspension, I asked Carrie Hofmann and the HR lady why I wasn't questioned during the investigative processes. They informed me that they talked to whom they needed to talk to but refused to tell me who. I asked why I didn't get a verbal or written warning, seeing as it was my first time being accused of having a bad tone. And the letter read, this is a final warning. The HR lady said my tone was so egregious in nature that it warranted an immediate suspension.

A few days after this incident and the drafting of the suspension letter, I filed my charge of discrimination against the station on June 1, 2016. I knew that I did not have a voice or an ally within the station or the company, so my only hope at protecting my livelihood was to get an outsider to hear my story.

Following the suspension, I would be chastised about the tone of my voice again—the tone of an e-mail and accused of not being open to constructive criticism. This had me literally walking on eggshells every day. I was mindful to pitch my stories in the daily editorial meetings but to not fight too hard because I didn't know when my tone would become offensive to my white female bosses. In an e-mail to management in 2017, I wrote, "It's disappointing that I can no longer have a discussion, explain my work, or simply disagree with my superiors without fear of reprisal." Unfortunately, this e-mail complaining about my work environment did not result in an independent investigation or any change for that matter.

In fact, this e-mail was never even discussed. They got the e-mail and never even spoke to me about it. That's just how irrelevant and invisible I was to the decision-makers at KSHB-TV.

In my opinion, the station made its first attempt to fire me following the bogus suspension for the tone of my voice in July of 2015. I called in to care for my sick son. That morning, manager, Carla Kreegar, took my call but somehow forgot to send the e-mail, notifying management staff. I was due to come to work at eight thirty in the morning. At 8:32 a.m., I got a phone call from a New Jersey phone number as I was sitting in the doctor's office with my son. When my son was taken back, I checked the voice mail. The voice mail was from the assistant news director, Mike Curtis's, personal cell phone. He left me a voice mail saying that he was expecting me at work. I knew immediately that a no call, no-show after my suspension would justify them firing me. After all, the letter said my job was in serious jeopardy. I immediately called Carla at the station, and the assignment manager said she was in Carrie's office and sent my call to her office. As I explained the situation to Carrie Hofmann, she told me that she had not talked to Carla and immediately gave me the excuse that Carla must have forgot to send the e-mail. She didn't know that I already knew that Carla was sitting in her office. To me, this was proof that they were working to get me out of the newsroom. When I inquired further, no one could explain why the assistant news director called me from his personal New Jersey cell phone versus his desk phone or his work cell phone. Yet again, there were no answers or investigations. We just moved on, and I continued to work in this toxic environment, paranoid that one day, they were going to finally figure out a reason to get rid of me, but not today.

My attorney was limited in the years he could refer to, but he went on to ask me about the jobs I applied for while at KSHB-TV.

Specifically, the investigative reporter position that Carrie Hofmann told me she wanted someone with data mining experience in an investigative unit. She told me she needed an experienced investigator because she wanted to get the story count up, and she wanted someone who could essentially hit the ground running and would not need to grow into the position. I, with my internalized racial inferiority, accepted that I wasn't qualified for yet another position. This, despite being an Emmy award-winning journalist. My attorney went on to show another e-mail from January of 2015, where I am again, essentially begging for an opportunity. I sat there, truly embarrassed in front of the jurors and my sisters. Why didn't I just leave this job? In the e-mail, in an effort to showcase my potential value in the investigative unit, I wrote, "I truly believe I would be an asset to the unit. I have contacts in the community and a desire to tell must watch stories that force accountability."

Shortly after the e-mail and the conversations with Carrie, she sent the HR lady an e-mail on June 10, 2015, and completely lied. She told the HR lady that I "wanted to do follow-up stories on yesterday's lead story. For example, if yesterday we covered a murder of a young child, she wanted to keep talking with family, go get more reaction, the latest on their investigation, etc. It was more about keeping current topics in the news, not uncovering wrongdoing. She said she didn't have experience with data gathering and document pulls to find stories."

Sitting in court, I was appalled at the blatant lie that Carrie e-mailed to HR because she did not want to consider me for the investigative reporter position. First, no general assignment reporter ever wants to keep going back to the grieving family members of murder victims. So why would I want to do that as an investigator? Second of all, data mining and document pulls were already part of my job. The reason Carrie gave me for disqualifying me is that I didn't have experience in an investigative unit. She clearly made up other excuses for HR and corporate to justify not promoting me into the position.

I then brought up to the jurors that Jessica McMaster's most successful investigation was initially a day-turn story about a missing

Kansas City, Kansas boy. McMaster turned the story of an abused and murdered child into a three-part investigation. In fact, McMaster ultimately won her first Emmy for that story. This after being hired as a reporter, who had no investigative unit experience and being allowed to grow into her position as an investigative reporter.

I went on to explain to the jurors how station management's commitment to find fault in my work solidified my resolve to document everything. At one point, Melissa Greenstein wrote new goals for me in the middle of the year. Each week, I would send an e-mail, entitled (goals met) to prove to her and everyone else that I was meeting my goals. The e-mails would detail my creative live shots, my story pitches of the week, and the only on exclusive content I produced. At no point did I ever get a response from management, but I knew if nothing else, I had indisputable evidence that I did my job week after week after week. At one point, my attorney asked me on the stand to explain why I was sending so many e-mails, and I told the jurors, "I'm e-mailing everything because I had situations in which Carrie would say something, and then she would act as though she didn't say it. So for me, I'm now having to memorialize every conversation and every exchange."

I didn't know if the jurors would understand this, but I know black people do. As a black woman, I am the imperfect victim. My words doubted, my actions criticized, and my motive always questioned. So I knew that the only way I would stand a chance against my white female bosses was to challenge them with their own words. This worked as far as proving my thoughts and actions during my time at KSHB-TV prior to trial, but Carrie ultimately stopped responding to my e-mails. In some situations, she would get my e-mail and walk out of her office and tell me to come talk to her in her office. She too knew that she would have to defend her typed words while the inconsistency of the words that fell from her mouth would automatically trump the facts that came from mine. In hindsight, it's clear that these white women know where their power lies; they just don't want others to acknowledge it for fear that exposure to the light would destroy it.

At this point, the defense counsel was still objecting to e-mails that he deemed as collateral issues. He told the judge, "Essentially, everything that displeases her and Mr. Egan is representing her at the time and we know that this is copied with his office. These are orchestrated attempts."

Again, he was trying to say this black woman is not intelligent enough to draft e-mails of this caliber without running them past her attorney. Clearly acting out of my own subconscious internalized racial inferiority, I was flattered that he thought so highly of my ability to slay words on paper. In my conscious mind, I was insulted that he assumed that I didn't have the intellectual ability to draft these e-mails on my own. This time, my attorney, Dennis Egan, set the record straight, saying, "I must say on record, I do resent the continued statement that this is all orchestrated by counsel. This lady can write and handle her own battles. These are all hers."

Score one for Team Lisa! I was so happy that my attorney disrupted the stench of racial superiority that was gushing from the defense attorney's mouth. He let everyone know that his client, a black woman, can, in fact, draft an e-mail and handle her own shit!

After a little more back-and-forth, my attorney moved on to my performance evaluations. He went over categories that spanned a number of years. His objective was to show the jurors my standard meets expectations and exceeds expectations and how evaluations changed to "does not meet expectation" after my 2015 EEOC complaint and the subsequent lawsuit.

My attorney soon brought up the time I was reprimanded for the tone of an e-mail. Again, this involved Melissa Greenstein, who had at that point been promoted to assistant news director. I told the jurors that I was working on a story, and I sent in my updates to let management and producers know what I was doing and what interviews we had. While using the voice to text feature on the phone, I said "efforting," but the phone typed "effing" in the e-mail. Within minutes, I corrected the typo and sent a corrected e-mail. Nonetheless, it was enough time for management to read the mistake, read the correction, and decide that the tone of the e-mail was inappropriate.

During the defenses' cross of me, he went crazy trying to get me to say that I typed "effing" because I really meant to say "fucking." Even in the story construction, it was clear in the e-mail that the expletive didn't even make sense. He was clearly trying to use this typo to distort my character and help the jurors see me as angry and vulgar toward management. From that incident, I got to explain how ridiculous the station was about overtime pay. They would expect us to stay late, come in early or work through lunch, but instead of paying us, we were expected to manipulate our time cards in favor of the station. This was something I had literally done since 2004 when I was hired. In this particular e-mail exchange, Melissa Greenstein was reprimanding me for not getting a lunch break on one of my MMJ days. An MMJ day is a day I was expected to set up, shoot, write, edit, and present my story on my own. Outside of stuffing a sandwich in your mouth while driving, I'd be willing to bet that most MMJs rarely get a real lunch break. "I consciously manipulated my days to avoid overtime. If I don't get a lunch break the next day, I may come in later or leave early on another day. The goal was to avoid charging overtime."

I went on to explain that in the rare times that I did charge overtime, I would be confronted with opposition from management, like they thought I was stealing from the company. A management style that left me and others working countless hours for free.

Overtime was the perfect transition to the newsroom and, more specifically, the MMJ hierarchy. I explained what an MMJ was now, and I got to explain who was burdened with the task of actually doing all that work by themselves, under deadline, while others enjoyed the partnership of an actual photographer.

I explained that all KSHB-TV reporters and anchors signed MMJ contracts, but who did the MMJing was completely up to management, which left some employees, many of them, people of color, doing the grunt work while other employees, including Christa Dubill and Jessica McMaster, consistently worked with photographers if they were in the field. I told the jurors about one particular incident when I was shooting a press conference at the Kansas City Missouri Police Department, and a white male reporter texted me questions and instructed me to ask them for his story. I told the court, "It was absolutely embarrassing and humiliating to be put into a position where I'm essentially working for my white coworkers who had far less experience than I did. But it was their way of letting everyone know where I, as a black woman and veteran journalist, sat on the hierarchy in the newsroom."

The inconsistencies of the MMJ hierarchy were discussed at length over the years at KSHB-TV among the minority reporters. There were some young white reporters who MMJ'd sporadically, but the lion's share of consistent MMJs were black employees. We had two black reporters for the four o'clock *The Now* show, who were expected to do it every day. Even the black anchors were expected to MMJ consistently outside of doctor's excuses or life-altering cancer diagnosis. It was pitiful and sad, but in not rocking the racial boat and protecting whiteness, we complained among ourselves and kept doing our jobs.

Shortly after a number of e-mails were admitted, the jurors went on break, and the attorneys went to battle on whether or not more documents could be admitted. One, specifically, was the commentary of the people on my personal Facebook page, who actually commented or reacted to the "White Tears" article. The defense counsel argued at the judge's bench that if she allowed that commentary that all the people who hated the article should be admissible. My attorney countered, saying I had no way of knowing that anyone hated the article because the haters weren't commenting on my personal Facebook page. My attorney, Dennis Egan, told the judge, referring to the comments on my page, "It's the only commentary that shows on her Facebook page. That's the relevance of it. We're talking about Lisa Benson who had no idea that she's offended Jessica McMaster and Christa Dubill. Their position is that they're terribly offended. This counters that and it is her Facebook and it remained that way."

The judge ruled that the comments on the page were hearsay because it was the statements that these people made regarding their opinions of the article for the truth of what their opinions are. However, she did allow my attorney to ask me if there were any negative comments on my page regarding the article.

When the jurors were escorted back into the courtroom, I was encouraged that I was on the homestretch. It was now after 3:00 p.m., and I only had a couple of more hours on the witness stand. We went over some of the stories that the jurors had already heard through the testimony of others, just to get my details and personal knowledge into the minds of the jurors. This included the incident with DelMeko Jordan where I was suspended for three days after an expletive got on air. This, despite that fact that he and another photographer actually edited the story and sent it to the station for air.

From there, we talked about preferred schedules and how the biases of my white managers meant that I would never get off weekends while the white employees with less experience would be deemed qualified for weekends off before their first week on the job. I sent an e-mail to HR in August of 2017 to bring the disparities to their attention. I sent this e-mail, knowing in my heart that their scheduling preferences were as deliberate as their MMJ scheduling. They wanted the white reporters to feel valued while the black reporters proved and reproved day after day that they deserved to even be there.

Nicole Eaton

From:	Benson, Lisa <Lisa.Benson@kshb.com>
Sent:	Friday, August 18, 2017 11:19 AM
To:	Winkler, Scott
Subject:	Schedule Privileges

Hi,
Thanks for listening to my concerns this morning.

This is a clip of the current reporter schedule. As you can see Cat Reid has already earned the "performance based" Monday through Friday dayside schedule.
Her start date was just 5 weeks ago, July 10th. She of course, is a white reporter.

Me, Steven Dial and Sarah Plake all continue to work the weekends. We are all minorities.

Just an FYI....Belinda Post, Charlie Keegan, Cat Reid, Tom Dempsey and Ariel Rothfield are ALL white reporters who have NEVER been assigned a weekend schedule.

Thanks again for listening,
~Lisa B.

Jade DeGood	PTO	4:30am - 12:30pm 4:30/7, traf 5-9	4:30am - 12:30pm Traffic	4:30am - 12:30pm Traffic	4:30am - 12:30pm Traffic	OFF
REPORTERS						
Belinda Post	3am - 1pm Reporter	3am - 1pm Reporter	3am - 1pm Reporter	3am - 1pm Reporter	3am - 1pm Reporter	OFF
Charlie Keegan	3am - 1pm Reporter	3am - 1pm Reporter	3am - 1pm Reporter	3am - 1pm Reporter	3am - 1pm Reporter	OFF
Andres Gutierrez	9:30am - 6:30pm Eclipse	9:30am - 6:30pm MMJ	9:30am - 6:30pm Reporter	1:30pm - 10:30pm Reporter	1:30pm - 10:30pm Reporter	On-Call
Cat Reid	9:30am - 6:30pm Reporter	9:30am - 6:30pm Reporter	9:30am - 6:30pm Reporter	9:30am - 6:30pm Reporter	9:30am - 6:30pm Reporter	OFF
Steven Dial	OFF	OFF	9:30am - 6:30pm MMJ	9:30am - 6:30pm Reporter	9:30am - 6:30pm Reporter	10am - 7 pm Reporter
Sarah Plake	4:00am - 7:00pm Eclipse	9:30am - 6:30pm Reporter	9:30am - 6:30pm Reporter	9:30am - 6:30pm Reporter	OFF	OFF
Alyssa Donovan	9:30am - 6:30pm Reporter	9:30am - 6:30pm Reporter	9:30am - 6:30pm Reporter	OFF	OFF	4:30am - 2:30p Reporter
Lisa Benson	OFF	9:30am - 6:30pm Reporter	9:30am - 6:30pm Reporter	9:30am - 6:30pm MMJ	9:30am - 6:30pm Reporter	1:30-10:30pm Reporter
Tom Dempsey	9:30am - 6:30pm Reporter	9:30am - 6:30pm Reporter	PTO	PTO	PTO	OFF
Ariel Rothfield	2:00pm - 11:00pm Reporter	2:00pm - 11:00pm Reporter	2:00pm - 11:00pm Reporter	2:00pm - 11:00pm Reporter	2:00pm - 11:00pm Reporter	OFF
WEATHER						

Lisa Benson
General Assignment/MMJ Reporter| 41 Action News

EXHIBIT NO. 75
ARPINO & BIGGS

1

In January of 2017, the station hired Jeff Mulligan, a black man, as the dayside executive producer. He immediately became my direct supervisor. I think it was Carrie's attempt to have a black person over me so she could cease communications all together. From the beginning, I tried to keep a distance from Jeff because I knew it was in his interest to feel about me the way that his bosses felt about me regardless of whether or not I was a good reporter or not. I told the jurors, "We didn't have any problems with each other. There was just low engagement from him because I'm still his employee that they wanted to get rid of. I'm still the employee that filed this grievance." I went on to tell the jurors that, at this point, people in the newsroom, especially people of color, were trying to distance themselves from me because they didn't want to be seen as sympathetic for fear of being treated as an accomplice.

My attorney went over a review where Mulligan made a comment about me not having characters in my story. And when I asked him to give me a specific example of a characterless story, he couldn't. Then we talked about Mulligan commenting about movement in my live shots. I explained to the jurors that as reporters, we are baptized in the ideology of demonstrative live shots and the proverbial walks to nowhere. But sometimes, there is nowhere to go and nothing to show to the viewer. I told the jurors that I admitted to not having anywhere to move on some of my live shots; therefore, that was an area that I was constantly working on. But in contrast, I told them that I always looked for characters in my story so that we don't have just a bunch of officials or talking heads.

I told the jurors, "When I'm knocking on doors trying to get people to talk to me, I'm looking for the characters or people who are affected by whatever issue…whatever I'm talking about. I want someone to share their story and how this topic affects them. So I'm very sure that in every single story, I find characters to support the story."

I hoped the jurors believed my testimony and that the reason Mulligan couldn't give me any examples of a characterless story is because he didn't have any.

We continued going over the review line by line with the jurors listening, including the portion of the review that Mulligan agreed to change after I challenged his evaluation of my work. We went by that topic quickly, but I hope the working-class jurors in the courtroom could understand the violation of a manager writing down a criticism of you and your work, and you being able to prove them wrong. Instead of looking for the good in you and lifting you up, your manager is literally making up stuff to devalue your work, and it's your job to come into your review, trying to win back points. That's exactly what I was having to do under my management staff at KSHB-TV.

From that conversation, we went to an e-mail from a white male producer who was giving me accolades for a story that I'd done. The e-mail said, "That story was awesome, and it's great to see that you're leading the way in covering stories that don't just hit dumb JOCO." JOCO was an abbreviation for Johnson County, a more affluent, predominantly white part of our coverage area. Me reading that part of the e-mail lead to a long objection by the defense counsel that lead to my attorney withdrawing the exhibit. The defense counsel didn't want the jurors to interpret the e-mail as saying the station has a preference for a certain area of coverage, which happened to be majority white.

I also told the jurors that I did believe that other employees in the newsroom did value me in their words, actions, and e-mails. It was simply management staff, who also happened to be the decision-makers, who saw no value in me, and frankly, I had no power to change their biases against me.

Next up, my attorney introduced the front page of my professional Facebook page, followed by a number of questions about the type of stories I covered for KSHB-TV. He quickly focused the questions so I could tell the jurors that I'd done a lot of race-based and race-related stories during my employment at the station. Then my attorney admitted four race-related television news video clips that I'd done at the station.

The defense objected to my attorney admitting the race-based stories, saying the stories were irrelevant and confused the issue for the jurors while my attorney was trying to make me a champion of race-based issued. My attorney defeated that argument, saying the stories were an example of my work. And the opinions in the stories were very similar to what was in the article I was terminated over. He told the judge that this was racially controversial information that went on the air at KSHB-TV and was approved by management.

The judged agreed, saying, "Given the issues in this case and given the issue of whether or not the article that was posted was an opinion, was inflammatory, was newsworthy, I do believe that these four exhibits are appropriate."

My attorney played several stories for the jurors. One entitled, "White Privilege Conference," another about unconscious biases, and another about a white supremacist who threatened to visit a local bookstore.

After finishing the racially charged videos, my attorney quickly marched the jurors to May 9, 2018. The day I shared the "White Tears" article on my personal Facebook page. I told the jurors about a normal routine Wednesday night of getting off work, eating dinner with my family, reading to my boys before putting them to bed, and relaxing at home. I told the jurors that some nights, my husband and I watched TV, or I'd read something, and this particular evening, I started piddling around on Facebook and stumbled across an interesting article in my news feed.

My attorney subtly steered the conversation to whom shared the story that lead to it popping up on my Facebook feed. I told the jurors it was Lora McDonald. Lora was the executive director of the Metro Organization for Racial and Economic Equity. I'd known her for years and had done countless stories with her in the community. But the part of her background that my attorney wanted the jurors to know is that she is, in fact, a white woman. A white woman who read the article and shared it because she too found interest in it. What the jurors may not have known is that redheaded white woman was also sitting in the courtroom.

When my attorney asked if Lora was a white woman, the defense immediately objected, but the judge overruled the objection, allowing me to answer the question. I told the jurors, "She's a Caucasian woman, a white woman."

I went on to tell the jurors how I read through three-fourth of the online article to where there was a video clip embedded in the webpage. Once I got to the video, I shared the article on my personal page with the intent of sharing it with others and conjuring it up on a personal computer later to watch the video. I told the jurors that I had an older phone at the time, and I questioned if the video would play properly. My attorney then asked me if I intended at the time to send something inflammatory out to my Facebook friends, and I said no.

I went on to explain to the jurors that the part of the article that resonated with me personally was the tone policing that was mentioned in the piece because I had already been suspended for the tone of my voice in May of 2015. I went on to explain that because I didn't understand why my tone was so offensive, the suspension made me desperate for answers. And this article provided some answers. I told the jurors about the conversations I initiated with the HR director about tone policing after finding articles online about tone policing—online articles that the HR director never engaged in conversations with me about.

I wasn't accused of violating the social media policy when I was initially suspended, but that was something the defense counsel was trying to prove in court. They pointed to an e-mail sent by the digital director as proof of a violation. The e-mail said that journalists have a responsibility to keep our opinions out of our work and out of the public eye, including social media. The article went on to say that a reporter can retweet a post or tweet because that's simply an act of reporting the news, but don't add anything, which is exactly what I did. I shared the article without comment and without liking it. I went on to explain to the courts that despite finding interest and great value in Ruby Hamad's article, it was not my opinion; it was her work.

"That was Ruby Hamad's article from *The Guardian*, which in my mind is a reputable news organization. Ruby Hamad is a journalist. I did find her article interesting, so I didn't see any problem in sharing her work," I said.

Kent's social media guidelines e-mail even included a social media no-no that was an example for reporters.

The almost comedic contradiction of the e-mail and the accusation is that the digital director, Kent Chaplain, who drafted the e-mail, violated his own guideline a month before I posted the "White Tears" article. He favored an opinion piece from *The Guardian* from his

Twitter account, a social media violation my legal team found during his initial deposition.

The article he favorited was entitled, "The NFL's Plan to Protect America from Witches." It was authored by Kareem Abdul-Jabbar. The article included a passage that read,

> The NFL's anachronistic fancies aren't just a misguided attempt to pander to what they think their traditionalist fans want, but also projects the hard-core conservative values of the mostly rich, white one-percenters who own the teams. We must live in their Disneyland or else.

Since the "White Tears" article was the crux of my termination at KSHB-TV, my attorney had me go line by line to explain to the courts which part of her article I agreed with and which parts were not in line with my own personal experiences. I was very careful in doing this because as a woman of color, I did not want to discount the experiences of another woman of color for the entertainment of the jurors or the courts. I absolutely believed that the experiences of the women highlighted in the article were their real, lived, life experiences. Some I had too experienced. Some I had not, yet.

I told the jurors that I cry when I don't want to cry, so with that, I don't know if people use tears strategically. They may or may not. I went on to share that growing up in my father's home, tears were punished with comments like, "If you keep crying, I'll give you something to cry for." I told them that growing up with that upbringing, I believed that tears were a show of weakness, so even when I am brought to tears, I immediately want to hide or isolate myself until they stop—something that happened a number of times in my life, including during my time at KSHB-TV.

I explained to the jurors that part of my interest in the article was that some found power in their tears because of what the tears signified and how others respond to them.

From that point, my attorney read several paragraphs from the article referring to a panel exchange at the Sydney Writers Festival, which read in part,

> In other words, the woman saw a personal attack where there wasn't one and decided to remind the panelists that as a member of the white majority, she ultimately has their fate in her hands.
>
> "I walked out of that panel frustrated," Ibrahim wrote. "Because yet again, a good convo was derailed, white people centered themselves, and a POC panel was told to police it's [sic] tone to make their message palatable to a white audience."

I quickly gave the jurors the personal connection I had to the words in the article. I told them that following my May 2015 conversation with Melissa Greenstein about file video, we never talked about the file video again. Instead, the subsequent conversations were about the tone of my voice and how it made this white woman feel.

Section by section, line by line, my attorney had me dissect Ruby Hamad's words to give the jurors my opinion in place of hers. In many areas, I staunchly agreed with Hamad. In other areas, I had to tell the jurors that those were Hamad's experiences and those of the women featured in her article.

At one point, I told the court, "I don't believe words are violence. I believe that as Americans, there is a freedom of speech. There's a freedom of the press. We should be able to speak to one another. We should be able to write our feelings and our unique experiences and not be considered offensive." I ended by saying that I thought that we as journalists should be the ones supporting these dialogues.

I was trying to get the jurors to see the bias and short-sightedness of both Christa and Jessica in not being willing to initiate and engage in a conversation if they found the article offensive. I wrapped up this line of questions with my attorney by reminding the jurors once again that Ruby Hamad's experience was not my lived experience, and as women of color, we are not monolithic. But I absolutely found truth and value in her work.

While I was resolute in making sure that I did not discredit Hamad's work, in all honesty, I was still centering whiteness in my answers. I consciously did not want to piss off the seven white jurors with my acknowledgment of where the power lies in the racial dynamic that exists between women of color and white women. I was worried about how much of my majority white jury understood that white people oftentimes see people in marginalized communities as part of a group, not as individuals. I was hoping that Hamad's Middle Eastern ancestry would distance us enough in their white minds that they would allow me as a black woman to have my own thoughts and opinions.

My attorney continued with rapid-fire questions about the article to embed my opinions and views into the minds of the jurors. I was especially encouraged when, after explaining my views of the article to the jurors, I was able to say, "I've never seen any of my coworkers cry."

I thought that was so relevant because it's not like we were dealing with a bunch of crybabies in the newsroom. These women were strong, leaders of their families, and go-getters in their careers. And I had never seen any of these women, my news director, or my assistant news director cry. So why in the world would any of them associate this article with my work at KSHB-TV? It made no sense unless it was a power play that they knew would work, much like the one highlighted in Ruby's article,

> "White women tears are especially potent... because they are attached to the symbol of femininity," Ajayi explains. "These tears are pouring out from the eyes of the one chosen to be the prototype of womanhood; the woman who has been painted as helpless against the whims of the world. The one who gets the most protection in a world that does a shitty job overall of cherishing women."

> Likewise, white women are equally aware their race privileges them as surely as ours condemns us. In this context, their tearful displays are a form of emotional and psychological violence that reinforce the very system of white dominance that many white women claim to oppose. (Ruby Hamad)

In my opinion, what was more likely in my situation is that this was a way for Jessica to get me out of the newsroom because she was tired of seeing my black ass after she got sucked into my discrimination lawsuit. And this was an opportunity for Christa to exert her main anchor power in the newsroom by helping her bosses get rid of the black woman who dared to file a racial discrimination lawsuit that made white people uncomfortable. And surely, she knew that her efforts and white solidarity would be rewarded when it came to contract and promotion talks.

My attorney was very detailed in highlighting poignant parts of the article. One of the most powerful for me that I hoped resonated with the jurors was this one,

> Whether angry or calm, shouting or pleading, we are still perceived as the aggressors. (Ruby Hamad)

I told the jurors I did have experience with that viewpoint. I hoped that they saw that it was playing out in the courtroom right before their eyes. From the defense attorney's description of me in opening statements to my coworkers testifying to being afraid of me. It was painfully clear that no matter what I did, in the eyes of my white counterparts and superiors, I was angry, aggressive, and unfit to be employed at KSHB-TV.

My attorney eventually transitioned to May 11, 2018. I was on paid time off, or PTO, when I got the call saying I was suspended. I didn't go into detail of why I was on PTO because it was irrelevant to the story, but it was priceless to me.

One of my former parent friends at my son's pre-K school invited me to a self-care workshop on May 10 at the Uzazi Village in Kansas City. I had never been in the space or attended a self-care workshop, but I was open to it because the stress of my situation was getting to me. From a lack of focus to interrupted sleep, to eye-twitching, I was definitely feeling the toll of a now three year journey to justice as a wife and mother of two young boys.

I was actually supposed to go to a meeting to dig up a few story ideas, but for some reason, I knew I needed to get some tools to better deal with stress. It was raining that night, and I remember running into the Uzazi Village and immediately being calmed by the tranquility and calmness of the space. The night included great conversation, connections with other black working moms, and a stress assessment. I scored ridiculously high on the test. Later in the evening, the therapist called for meditation. For people who believe in God, like myself, meditation included prayer. I sat there and prayed to God about my job, this lawsuit, and what to do about the results of my stress test. Based on the physical manifestations of the stress according to the test, I should be concerned. I clearly remember lying on the floor quietly with my eyes closed, after my prayers, and the Lord speaking to me, saying, "This chapter must end." I rebutted God in the spirit immediately. "God, it can't end now. I'm not going to quit. If I quit, I throw the lawsuit. I've come too far to stop now.'

I lay there until the mediation ended and thanked our host for having us. On my way out the door, it was still raining, and I remember getting in the car and saying again in my mind, "I'm not going to quit. I've come too far to quit. I have to finish this." On my way home, as kind of a concession to God and an acknowledgment that I wasn't okay, I called KSHB-TV and told the nightside manager that I had to take care of some personal things, and I needed to take a PTO day the next day, May 11.

He said, "Okay, I hope everything is okay." I said thank you and got off the phone.

The very next morning, after dropping my kids off at school, I missed a phone call from Scott Winkler, the HR guy. I called him back immediately, and it went to voice mail. Within minutes, he called me again. This time, I answered, and he told me the station had gotten some internal complaints, and they were suspending me for creating a hostile work environment based on race and sex.

I was shocked. I think the first thing I said was, "You're suspending *me* for creating a hostile work environment." I was taken aback because my initial complaint included hostile work environment that was later dropped by the judge.

I asked Winkler a few questions; none of which he answered. It was like he was reading a script. He repeated the same words back to me and told me that I would be contacted by an outside investigator. After getting off the phone with Winkler, I kept wondering what in the world I could have done to someone. Since he said race and sex, I thought sexual. Did I make a comment? Did someone lie and say I touched them inappropriately? I was confused.

I immediately called my attorney's office and told them, which started a more than a weeklong waiting game to figure out what I did and who I offended. While waiting for word on why I was suspended, I was suddenly locked out of my company e-mail on May 14, which I was still accessing through my phone. Immediately, after getting the notification that I didn't have access to my work e-mail, I just knew that this was it. I was being fired. I told my attorney, which launched yet another e-mail, to figure out what was going on. Ultimately, the station argued that it was just time to reset my password, which is why the system kicked me out. They eventually granted me access to my e-mails again, but we never believed their excuse.

KSHB-TV's Independent Investigator

On Friday, May 18, 2018, I finally got to meet the investigator hired to look into the allegations against me. Ann Molloy was a middle-aged white woman, so I knew from the beginning that I would have an uphill battle. But once she showed me a screengrab of the article and the meme that lead to my suspension, I legitimately thought I had a shot. A shot at convincing this white woman that me reading and sharing an article on Facebook did not negatively affect the work environment at KSHB-TV. Clearly, I was wrong.

The brunette, who appeared to be in her mid to late forties, passed two pieces of paper across to me while sitting at a table in my attorney's office. Finally, I knew what I was accused of doing wrong. I was being accused of reading and disseminating information that white people did not like—specifically, two white women at my job. Molloy took notes as she asked me questions about the article and the meme. I wondered why she didn't record the exchange because I knew it would leave everything up to her interpretations. I was encouraged by my attorney sitting in on the proceedings, but I still questioned how objective her final report would be, seeing as E. W. Scripps was paying her a lot of money.

I remembered having a pretty straightforward, candid conversation with Molloy about my reading and posting of the article, about the *Black Panther* meme, and how I thought Jessica McMaster's problem with me started before I read the article. She appeared to be listening and even agreeable at some points in regards to the content of the article. But this experience made me so distrusting of seemingly nice white people that I couldn't put anything past her affirming nods and faint smile. I expected her to move in solidarity with the white women who had already decided I should lose my job for daring to read and share an article that put white people in a less-than-favorable light.

After seeing Molloy's notes, I was right. Her shorthand reflected a pattern of my words and thoughts that she wanted to highlight and ignored others. I was surprised to see in her notes and report that she agreed the "White Tears" article "in and of itself is interesting," and "it is of value for the information it offers."

She went on to write in her final report that "under different circumstances, and in a different forum, the article might have provided a basis for discussion and dialogue." She didn't say what that different forum would be, if not my personal social media account. In her report, she also concluded that my sharing of the article did not create a hostile work environment but added that it did run contrary to the principles established in Scripps' Social Media Policy, which was a shock to me because I hadn't been accused of violating a social media policy, but again, it was clear they were just trying to find any excuse to get rid of me. And while the evidence against me did not support their accusations against me, she was clearly trying to give them another way to justify terminating me.

My attorney's questions then went to June 12, 2018, the day I was officially terminated from my job at KSHB-TV at a hotel in the Country Club Plaza. I distinctly remember receiving a call from Scott Winkler, the HR guy, who told me the investigation into my suspension had concluded and to meet them at the hotel. I asked him directly if I was being fired. He refused to answer. My husband and I were sharing one car at the time, so he drove me to the hotel. As I quietly took the short ride to the hotel, part of me knew that my life was about to change. I was sad, but I didn't want my husband to see me cry because I didn't want him to know how afraid I was to really live solely under his provisions as a self-employed entrepreneur. And my entire being knew that no matter what happened, I would not give my superiors the option of being entertained and validated by my tears.

I arrived at the hotel a few minutes before our appointed time and was waiting for my attorney when Winkler greeted me and told me to come back to a conference room they had reserved in the back. I told him I was waiting for my attorney, but he told me my attorney could not sit in on the proceedings, so I followed him back to the room and took a seat. The general manager, Steve Watt, and the dayside executive producer, the black guy, Jeff Mulligan, were already in the room. Of course, they would send the black guy to balance out the room.

Watt started reading from my termination letter, and the only part that stuck with me was when he said, "I was not to return to work."

Once he finished reading the letter, I tried to say as little as possible because I knew that no matter how unfair it was, or what it was going to cost me as far as my family, my income, my family's insurance, that I would not have a voice in this space no more than I had a voice in the newsroom or with E.W. Scripps.

So, at this point, I was more concerned with being able to walk in and out with my dignity intact. As I shared my innermost feelings with the courts, I was literally falling apart on the stand. I was like really ugly crying. Despite grabbing tissue after tissue, I could not stop my own tears. I was honestly surprised at how much it hurt to talk about the moments leading up to losing my career and losing my livelihood. And for some reason, even sitting there, I was ashamed of my tears. I was ashamed of my weakness. It also reminded me of a passage in the "White Tears" article that I will never forget. "Brown and black women know we are imperfect victims…and we know that against a white woman's accusations, our perspectives will almost always go unheard either way."

I knew that despite my obvious pain at confronting the discrimination, retaliation, and harassment I had endured at KSHB-TV, there was a pretty good chance my jurors couldn't hear my voice because I too was an imperfect victim.

In an effort to help me compose myself, my attorney asked me about other parts of the termination letter, including my delayed tax filings. I explained to the jury that as of my termination date, my taxes were filed, and I told the GM that, but it had no effect on their decision to terminate me. I also asked the men in the room if I could come up to the station and get my things. The HR director reminded me again that I was not allowed on property and said they would catalog and mail my things to my home.

In hopes of educating the jurors, my attorney had me explain the ramifications of my not being able to go to the station and get hard or digital copies of my work. It meant that I could not create a new résumé tape to market myself as a reporter to another station. I told the jurors, "When you talk about broadcast companies in the top 30 markets, they're going to want a high-quality example of your recent work. Without access to the station and my stories, I can't create a quality video résumé."

I even went so far as to explain how a résumé tape is formatted to showcase anchoring and reporting. I was hopeful that the jurors could see how deliberate I thought E. W. Scripps was in denying me access to my recent stories. I went on to tell the jurors that I had sent out paper résumés to stations here in Kansas City, but I hadn't gotten so much as a phone call or e-mail.

From there, my attorney got back into the real-life cost of me losing my job. I told the jurors that I'd been a television news reporter since the age of twenty-two, and without access to my work to make a résumé tape with my recent work, it would be hard to reemerge at a station in Kansas City or any other place in the country for that matter. I told the jurors it was like trying to redefine yourself and your career at a time in your life when women were considered less hirable, less desirable. I was in my early forties. To be honest, it was a little embarrassing for people to still recognize me from my work at the station and for me to have to tell complete strangers that I no longer work there, and in many instances, why. From there, my attorney asked me about the significance of my income in my household. In addition to crying again about the price of insurance, I told the jurors my husband was self-employed for the majority of our marriage, so I'd always been the consistent breadwinner at our house. I fought back tears as I said, "I was the primary breadwinner, and everybody was on my insurance, so it worked for us, so once I lost my job, we didn't have the consistent income anymore."

I also told the jurors that is was because of the flexibility of my husband's schedule that I was able to report to work at four o'clock in the morning on Saturdays and Sundays for several years despite having young children at home. My husband's career path supported the crazy work schedule and hours that were expected of me at KSHB-TV.

Parts of this conversation about my household finances and my taxes were embarrassing to me, and it felt a little bit like trauma pimping. I knew my attorney thought it would be impactful for the jury to see the emotional toll this experience had on me as an employee, wife, and a mother. But I couldn't help but resent that I was now hoping these seven white jurors would see my tears, feel sorry for me, and punish my employer. When in my heart, I didn't want pity. I wanted to knock the jurors over the head with the reality of racial inequities, the burden of racial ignorance, and the power of white privilege.

Following a few questions about pay disparities and the fact that my white coworkers make a lot more money than I did, we recessed for the day, which was a Friday. This meant I would be back on the stand on Monday to face my cross-examination by the defense counsel.

Before we headed home for the day, the judge reminded both sides of their time restraints and how much time each side had left. My attorney also lobbied to get another KSHB-TV news story admitted, where the NAACP president says, "White supremacy is in our DNA." The judge ultimately ruled against allowing the video, saying it was cumulative.

I remember walking to my car at the end of the week completely exhausted. I could not believe this was happening, including the lies about me and my character that were bounced around in the courtroom. We could not have cameras in the courtroom, but I knew I wanted my voice to be heard as we sat in trial without any interest from the local television stations and limited interest from the local newspaper.

I decided I would do a Facebook post, summarizing my experiences in court so that my supporters and friends would know what's going on. On Sunday evening, I did a Facebook post about the lies they told in court and the racial composition of the jury. Personally, I thought the post was eloquent and powerful. I paralleled the racial stereotypes and biases used against me in court by E. W. Scripps to the ones used to subconsciously justify the killing of twelve-year-old Tamir Rice. A white police officer killed Tamir in 2014 as he was playing with a toy gun on the playground. The white officer believed he was in danger the minute he saw Tamir's brown skin. Despite the fact that he was a child at a playground playing with a toy.

Within minutes, I got an enraged call from my attorney, telling me to take my Facebook post down. I took it down immediately, but I was angry that I had not been instructed by my legal team not to post on social media. As a journalist, I was accustomed to asking inappropriate questions to tell other people's stories. So now I felt somewhat obligated to be transparent in sharing my journey. In subsequent conversations, my attorney was furious about the post and feared that the defense would use it to contaminate the case or force a mistrial. I was worried and terrified that I had inadvertently messed up my own case. I had to wait until Monday morning to see what the judge would do with my social media misstep.

CHAPTER 9

Week Two of Trial

First thing Monday morning, my attorney informed the judge of my Facebook post that stayed up for less than twenty minutes. The defense counsel didn't see it, but it didn't stop them from trying to make an issue of it. We produced a copy of the text from the post, but it didn't include the pictures. And since I deleted the post itself, we couldn't figure out how to revive it. The judge instructed the jurors to tell the court if they saw or read anything about the case. Thankfully, none of the jurors responded. The worry of the possibility of this affecting the case loomed for a couple of days. But eventually, the judge said it was a moot point because none of the jurors or the defense counsel saw it. Thank God! I was still a little standoffish toward my attorneys, following the incident because of how condescending they were toward me about the post. But eventually, I got over it and focused on presenting well before the jurors so they would hopefully believe me.

It was Monday morning on the second week of my trial, and attorneys on both sides were going at it. My attorney wanted to show the jurors that after posting the "White Tears" article on my personal Facebook page, I didn't receive any negative comments. Therefore, how would I know that anyone was offended? The defense counsel wanted to introduce the negative comments about the article from TheGuardian.com website to prove that there were other people who did not like the article. The judge did not allow the defense counsel to introduce comments from the TheGuardian.com website. The judge allowed my attorney to ask me if there were negative comments on my Facebook page about the article. The answer to that question was no.

Snow and potential ice storms tormented my trial. At various points, we feared that we'd have to leave early or delay court because of weather. On day one of week two, the judge assured the jurors that they were monitoring the weather to keep everyone safe on their commutes home.

I was sworn in again. My attorney asked me about the passion I had for my job as a television news reporter despite my discrimination claim. I told the jurors that "I wanted to be heard. I wanted them to consider what I was going through, but I absolutely enjoyed what I did. I loved my career."

Sitting there, saying those words to the jury, I could remember when it was true. But somewhere between applying for jobs that I knew I wasn't going to get, filing an official grievance, and being treated like I was something "other" than a professional journalist who happened to be black, I definitely fell out of love with the job. I, instead, became focused on the mission. I wanted to force my superiors to see me and hear my voice. If that meant two weeks in a federal courtroom and millions of dollars in attorney fees for E. W. Scripps—run it!

My Cross-Examination

My attorney finished asking me questions and then handed me over to the defense counsel for cross-examination. The attorney approached very pleasantly but quickly began talking fast as he asked me question after question.

I remember thinking about each question and answering them somewhat timidly because I feared each question was some sort of trick. He covered very little new ground but seemed to restate topics in hopes of confusing me or manipulating my words. The defense attorney played snippets of my videotaped deposition in hopes of catching me in a contradiction. But honestly, even when he attempted to impeach my testimony with my own deposition, I could not figure out where the contradiction was. When referring to my conversation with Melissa Greenstein, he kept accusing me of "yelling" at my boss. At several points, he started his question with, "Isn't it true you were angry when you..." fill in the blank. He was squarely focused on my angry black woman rage in hopes of convincing the jurors that my white bosses and coworkers had reason to fear me and ultimately get rid of me.

The defense attorney also asked me about applying for weekend anchor positions and how I applied for them. I explained to him in some instances I took a physical résumé tape to the news director's office, and other times, I applied online through the company's website. And despite the fact that other coworkers, including Lindsay Shively and Dia Wall, admitted that they never applied for their promotions, the attorney repeated numerous times that I did not complete my online application process. An error he said that made me ineligible for the job.

At one point, he even asked me if I should have received an anchor position instead of the person who was hired. Believe it or not, even at this stage of self-awareness, it was hard for me to articulate that I deserved what I was asking for from this company. It felt like I was betraying my former coworkers by saying that I too deserved an opportunity, and I should have been hired for the one they were given. But I did it. I said yes.

From there, the defense counsel kept playing portions of my videotaped depositions and omitting others in hopes of painting me in a negative light in front of the jurors. Soon his questions focused on the "White Tears" article.

At one point, he asked me if there was anything I would do differently, and I told him, "If I had a magic wand and I could go backward, I would have my HR director or my boss call me and say, 'Hey, someone has a problem with that article you shared, would you mind taking it down.'" The defense objected to my answer, saying it was nonresponsive, but the judge allowed it.

Then he asked me if I could understand why any "reasonable" person could be offended by the article, and do you think that anyone who is offended by this article is unreasonable by your definition. His voice was elevated asking the questions, and he seemed visibly irritated by my answer when I responded saying something along the lines of "I don't know why anyone would be offended unless they employ these tactics." I continued, saying, "This article was posted by a white woman, and I shared it from a white woman's page. And the only person who commented on the article was another white woman. From my vantage point, there was no reason to believe that white women would be offended."

From there, I was able to restate my script I came up with for the deposition, which was, "This was a point of view article written by a woman of color about the racial dynamic that can exist between white women and women of color."

He asked me if I would have taken the article down if the girls had talked to me. I told him and the courts, "If someone saw it on my social media page and said it was offensive at the time, I would have taken it down. The point of me sharing the article was my interest, not to offend. It was to enlighten and promote dialogue. It's interesting."

Even answering that question, I knew, at that time, I would have taken it down in the interest of keeping my job, but now I would not. I would fully engage in a conversation about the alleged offense in hopes of helping someone else better understand the racial hierarchies that exist in our everyday lives.

Looking out into the galley at my friend, Lora McDonald, I had to keep reminding myself to slow down. I wasn't angered by his questions, but I was like a horse champing at the bit, ready to respond, but I knew that any level of passion could be interpreted as anger, so I had to calm down and slow down to make sure the jurors didn't see me as a threat.

After his cross-examination, which lasted the entire day, my attorney got to do redirect and clear up a few things. At this point, I felt like I was on the down slope. Just a few more hours, and I could take my seat again at the plaintiff's table and watch the rest of the show.

My attorney talked about the news special the station approved about the fiftieth anniversary of the Kansas City Race Riots done by Dia Wall. He quoted a statement out of the story, "Anybody who is satisfied with where we are is actually contributing to us becoming worse. Because the moment that we're no longer intentional about trying to improve race relations is the moment that we begin our reverse."

He was quoting Missouri Congressman Emanuel Cleaver's comment in the story. I think he did that as not only a reminder of the messages about racism KSHB-TV shared on air but also as a jolt to the jurors who would ultimately be deciding on a case smothered in racism.

Next, he quoted another statement from a story I did about the White Privilege Conference that was hosted in Kansas City. He read, "We need to talk about white privilege. We need to talk about the ways in which folks are shut off from economic opportunities that keep them poor, living sicker and shorter lives."

Again, this was without a doubt another reality check for the jurors and the defense counsel. Further proving that it wasn't controversial racial topics that were so offensive to my white coworkers at KSHB-TV. It was me, the black woman, who dared to sue the station and expose them to the access and privilege that came along with their white skin.

During my redirect, my attorney also reminded the jury that my general manager, Steve Watt, contradicted what he told the independent investigator when my job was on the line. I reminded the jurors that I was in the courtroom when Steve Watt said he didn't take the African proverb meme to denote violence, but he took it to mean that I wanted to go to trial. The defense objected to my attorney using the GM's own testimony to prove that he's a liar, but the court allowed it, and I told the jurors I felt that was more in line with the truth because this meme had nothing to do with my job at all, and I was surprised that he actually said during the investigation that it had anything to do with violence or how I felt about the station. It made me seem like I was a very aggressive, angry person when the meme was about the *Black Panther* movie. It was a great movie. I enjoyed the movie.

I truly appreciated my attorney creating space for me to not only explain the meme again but to make the station and upper management look foolish and frankly racist for drawing conclusions about me without so much as a conversation with me.

From there, my attorney continued to allow me to debunk the lies the defense counsel disseminated by playing sound bites from my videotaped depositions. And again, sitting there, I couldn't help but notice how easy it was for them to take pieces of my words and create whole lies to present before a panel of strangers employed to decide my case. I know as a journalist with more than twenty years of television news experiences, I never did that or wanted to paint someone in a negative light based on personal motives. But this trial made it painfully clear to me that journalists have the power to do just that, especially if they have a top down power structure that supports their personal biases or viewpoints. This power is why it is so important to have diversity in the newsroom. And this power is why there are very few people of color in middle and upper management positions in newsrooms across the country. The way I see it now, once you oppose the power structure, your opportunity for growth is limited because the people who support their views are going to be seen as having leadership potential. Those who oppose are seen as troublemakers, even if the opposition is in an effort to bring forth racial equity and truth in storytelling.

Before I left the stand, my attorney put my farewell Facebook posts up for the jurors to see. In the first one, I told viewers I was no longer an employee at the station. In the subsequent one, I wanted to clarify that I had not quit.

Page Settings

 Lisa Benson is 😊 feeling happy in **Kansas City, Missouri.** •••
Posted by Lisa Benson
June 13, 2018 · 🌐

Hey **Facebook** friends,
I've hit my final liveshot at KSHB-TV!
After 14 years and 3 months, I am no longer a reporter at **41 Action News - KSHB-TV.**
I can't thank you all enough for allowing me into your homes and trusting me to tell your stories.

From covering the inauguration of president **Barack Obama** to becoming an Emmy award-winning journalist...I will forever cherish my work here in Kansas City!
I'm not sure what's next for me careerwise, but I'm excited about spending more time with my family, especially my two little boys!
Thanks again for your support & let's keep in touch as I navigate my next chapter!

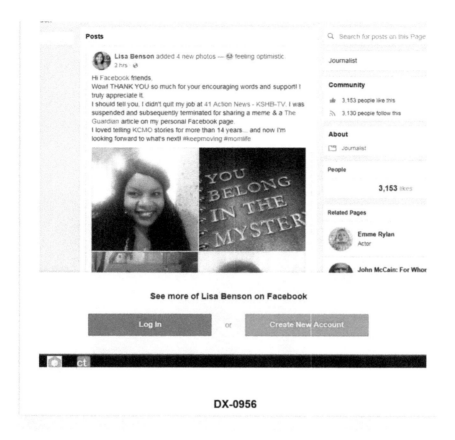

After my attorney read part of the post, I got the opportunity to explain why it was important for me to be transparent with viewers. One, I had nothing to hide, and I was terminated. Two, many of the people who followed me on my professional Facebook page connected with me through a story. I felt and still feel it would be beyond hypocritical of me to expect people to share their truth with me as a journalist but shut down when those same people inquire about my truth.

Then my attorney transitioned into the cease and desist letter the station sent me after I was terminated and my response. I remember receiving that letter via certified mail and freaking out. I could not believe the station was trying to take ownership of my Facebook account when I know they didn't do that with any of the others employees who left the station. In my response e-mail, I told the station I planned to keep my Facebook followers abreast of events going on in my career and life. I reminded them that I started my page in 2008, and it was not assigned to me by station management. I then went on to name former employees who still maintained ownership of their work Facebook accounts and asked why should I be treated any differently. The station did not respond to my response e-mail, and I continued using my professional Facebook account.

A huge part of my case that my attorney kept trying to establish, prove, and reprove was that I had complained about racial disparities before my May 2015 suspension through a company sponsored "EthicsPoint Hotline." The defense counsel fought to not allow the actual report of the call to be entered into evidence, so my attorney had me recollect my memory with the report from my call and tell the jurors why I called the line.

It was crazy to me how much my attempts at securing and working part-time jobs factored in. I briefly substitute taught while working and routinely would look for part-time jobs at airlines. Surely, the jurors had to understand that with my salary and changing family dynamics, more money was of great interest to me. This was especially true in 2015 when I realized that they were clearly trying to get rid of me. I always thought if I could get on part time with an airline, maybe I could transition into a full-time job when and if I got fired. The flight benefits were also of interest to me, as someone who loved to travel but never really had the income to do it as much as I'd like to.

I'll never forget the defense attorney pulling up a screengrab of a picture of my husband and I having breakfast the day after I was fired. My husband took me to the Classic Cup Café on the Plaza, which is the same location where he proposed to me over breakfast in 2007.

My husband took a picture of us smiling and added a caption about his "girl finally being home" and posted on his Facebook page. The defense counsel made issue of the fact that I was smiling in the picture after being terminated. So much so that on recross my attorney asked me if I was a person who normally frowned in pictures. It was ridiculous, but my emotional response to explaining our random breakfast was unexpected even for me. Tears raced down my face as I told the jurors, "When I was nonrenewed at Channel 41 News, I lost my career, my livelihood, I lost my income, and my family lost their insurance. I did not lose my life. Both of my parents had died by the time I was twenty-four years old, and I've covered countless murders and homicides and fatal accidents. So if you're asking me if I love life, absolutely! So I still have a reason to smile today."

In my cross-examination, the defense counsel referenced the seven-day cruise my husband and I took in April of 2018 for our tenth year anniversary and the post I made on Facebook. I could tell this was the defense's attempt to prove to this primarily working-class jury that I was another black woman who was trying to take advantage of the system to support my fiscally irresponsible, exuberant lifestyle. I mean, after all, I am black, so why should I be able to have the resources to enjoy something like a seven-day cruise? My attorney had to remind the jurors of the dates to prove that my April 2018 anniversary cruise preceded my June 2018 termination. He even had me ensure the jurors that since my termination, my family and I hadn't been anywhere outside of a local lake to take the kids fishing and to St. Louis to visit my family. He even made sure the jury knew that I stayed with my sister, seeing as we no longer had expendable income to pay for a hotel because I had been fired. Again, I went along with the poverty pimping because I knew it's what the jurors needed to believe me. They needed to see, feel, and believe my pain in order to feel sorry for me and see any credence in my lawsuit. Thanks to the research I was doing, I understood that white people have internalized white superiority, even the most well-meaning ones. So if the story the defense counsel painted of my life trumped the reality of theirs, there was no way I was going to get a favorable verdict. Knowing the reality of the anti-blackness culture I was born into, these white jurors were not going to reward a black person with money, whom in their eyes was already doing better than them.

My attorney knew this, and I subconsciously knew that as a college-educated black woman who owned her own home, was a frequent traveler, had a husband, and two healthy children, these working-class white jurors would think that I had already gotten more than I deserved. They too would decide in their subconscious bias riddled minds that I was lucky to be where I was, and I should be grateful.

I would guess a number of the jurors on my panel didn't even have a passport, so in getting jurors to reconnect with me though my pain and lack, my attorney reminded the jurors that the station's former general manager had just returned from New Zealand. Then he literally named every continent on the globe, starting with Australia and ending with South America and asked me if I'd been there. The answer to each question was a sad and somber "no." This was to prove to the jury that I was not a world traveler. For some unknown emotional reason, tears started flowing again as I, again, showcased my lack before a jury of my peers, in hopes of them believing that I had been discriminated and retaliated against at work. The painful truth is that public shame and humiliation is a true cost of litigation in the US Court system. Good thing, my mom raised me to live my truth and to not be ashamed of my decisions. There is nothing I've done that I'm not willing to talk about. And my time on the stand only proved that. The defense counsel tried to exploit a difficult time in my marriage in 2013 after my first son was born when my husband and I had separated. But thank God, I've been married long enough, and I've been to church enough to know that every test is a testimony in the making. When the defense tried to embarrass me into telling these complete strangers the intimate details of the trials in my marriage, I took the opportunity to minister about expectations and how they can be the death of marriage. I told the courts,

> I had expectations in marriage that were not met, and growing up as a young woman, you think marriage should look a certain way. It should feel a certain way. But once you marry someone, you marry that whole person. The good, the bad, the ugly. And you marry that person's whole family too. So there were times that I didn't get what I wanted out of the deal, but thanks to my church,

family, and friends, I realized that I had to give him the grace of his own humanity and room to grow in this marriage. He and I went into this marriage without perfect models, as far as what marriage was. Neither of us had perfect examples, so we definitely had some work to do to get to a place where we were loving each other properly. I had to give him space to be a human being who's flawed, and he had to give me grace for my imperfections as well. So I had to learn that expectations are hard on a marriage, and you have to simply give people room to grow.

Even typing these words today for this book, I am still a work in progress, and these words are ministering to me. I believe they spoke to the men on my jury panel, and I truly believe they fought for me in the deliberation room because they were moved by my honesty and my decision to protect my husband when the defense counsel wanted me to humiliate him and devalue our marriage and family.

Defense Recross

The defense recross garnered a lot of bench conversations because the defense attorney tried to admit a stack of negative comments about the "White Tears" article that were allegedly on TheGuardian.com website, that I had never seen or read. I reiterated multiple times that I did not receive any negative comments on my page about the "White Tears" article but they kept prodding me as though my testimony was not supported by the Facebook post that had already been admitted into evidence. My attorney kept stepping in, and eventually, the judge told him to move on. He could not enter into evidence the litany of negative comments he said were on TheGuardian.com website.

Next Up, Juror Questions for Me

In US Federal Court, jurors get to ask witnesses questions, and the same was true for me. After two and a half days of questions and answers, the jurors had a lot of questions. At the request of the defense counsel, the judge asked me to leave the room as both sides argued over which questions should or should not be asked.

As I sat in the small conference room waiting for my paralegal to tell me it was showtime again, I couldn't help but to rethink some of my answers and wonder what the jurors thought of me. When I walked off the stand, an older white juror smiled at me. So I knew that despite my blackness, I was breaking through on some level. But there were two middle-aged white women who showed no reaction to anything, so I definitely had reason to be worried.

I waited less than thirty minutes before our paralegal, opened the door, and told me it was time to take the stand again. The first question was, "During 2015 through now, did you look for employment elsewhere?

I explained to the jurors my contract had a noncompete clause in it. And under the rules of the contract in order for me to get another on-air job, I would have to quit KSHB-TV and sit out for six months without an income. I was glad the jurors asked the question because it showed the conundrum the station created for employees. Unlike other professions, I couldn't just start looking for a better job elsewhere without violating my contract or trying to live without an income for six months.

The jurors asked me about looking for part-time work with an airline and working part time as a substitute teacher in 2015 while still working full time at KSHB-TV. I was happy to explain to these fellow working-class folks that "there were other employees who were substitute teachers. They were the employees who were the lower earners, the lower earners were working part time." I wanted to explain to my jurors that part-time work was a necessity and a reality for a number of employees who worked at KSHB-TV, not just me. I even mentioned our weekend sports anchor, a black man, who also substitute taught to help supplement his income. I was hoping that the burden and real need to at times work two jobs resonated with the jurors.

The jurors also asked whether or not I was interviewed for an anchor position I applied for at a sister station in December in 2015. I boldly told the jurors, "No, I was never considered for an anchor position within E. W. Scripps family." I wanted them to know that in my fourteen-year tenure at the station, no one ever sat down with me and honestly considered me for promotion.

Another juror question asked, "Throughout your employment with 41 Action News, would you post articles that dealt with race on your personal Facebook page other than the Ruby Hamad article?" Again, I quickly answered yes to the question and named another article that I recalled at the time. In answering this question, I was hoping that the jurors were starting to see that the problem with me was not in me daring to share an article about systemic racism, it was me daring to hold KSHB-TV responsible for racial discrimination and disparities.

One of the most telling questions was about the four news stories that my attorney showed to the court to prove that KSHB-TV had covered tough topics about race. The question was, "Do you believe the four stories related to race issues that were shown to the jury may be seen as attacking or discriminating against a protected class?"

My answer, which I paused before answering was, "No. The reason is, as a news organization, we would often address very tough issues about racism and sexism. There were even situations in which I was used as an agitator if you will. In fact, the video you watched showed me at a bookstore where they were expecting a white suprem-acist author to show up. They selected me to go as the agitator. I would confront him, ask him questions, and the hope was that my mere presence as a woman of color would be an agitator."

I went on to talk about a previous reporting assignment where I was sent to the home of a known KKK member in 2009. This incident was omitted from evidence because it went too far back in time, but I thought this question was a perfect opportunity to share how KSHB-TV used my race to further their news gathering agenda when it served them.

I continued answering the same question, telling the jurors, "Another situation, I was sent to the home of a known KKK member by myself." Before I could finish the story, the defense attorney interrupted and asked the judge if they could approach the bench.

According to courtroom transcripts, the first thing the defense attorney said after I mentioned that I had been sent alone to the home of a known KKK member was a motion for a mistrial, "Move for a mistrial. We think this is absolutely prejudicial." He continued fuming at the bench, telling the judge, "This is her MO. This is her demeanor. She wants to advocate and be her own lawyer, and she responds to a simple question and tries to interject inflammatory issues to tar and feather us. If we lose this case, it's going to be because of this."

The judge responded, saying, "It is not grounds for a mistrial. Your request is denied."

Despite the defense counsel's obvious fire and fury over me mentioning the KKK incident, what he did not call me was a liar. He knew, just like KSHB-TV management knew, that my race was a factor in my hiring, my story assignments, and my lack of promotion. And they knew if the jurors saw the truth of what I experienced at that station, they would rule in my favor. That truth is, why the defense counsel would move full speed ahead with their vicious lies when they began presenting their case?

One of the questions that my attorney fought to not make me answer was about white privilege. The question, I would guess, was asked by one of the middle-aged white women was, "Do you feel all or most whites are considered 'white privileged?'"

The defense counsel wanted me to answer the question, but my attorney convinced the judge that since we were dealing with a mostly white jury, and it was a hot-button topic, answering the question honestly would work against me. My attorney told the judge that it was clear that a juror was taking this topic personally by the wording of the question. Thankfully, the judge agreed. In my mind, this is further proof that mainstream America needs to have more conversations about the reality of systemic racism and how it shows up in our everyday lives and in the laws and policies that govern this land. But since we're not having these conversations, white people choose to take a personal offense to the term "white privilege."

The judge asked me a handful of questions about contracts, tax returns, and me being locked out of my work e-mail while I was on suspension before I was finally allowed to leave the witness stand, and my attorney rested his case. Now I had a front row seat to watch the slander, disparaging remarks, and lies that would mold the defense's case in hopes of proving to this jury that I was unworthy of any opportunities for growth at KSHB-TV.

Immediately before presenting one witness, the defense counsel presented a motion for a directed verdict. A motion for a directed verdict is a motion arguing to the court that no reasonable jury could find for the opposing party; therefore, dismissing the case before the defense counsel presented their case. Thankfully, this tactic didn't work either. The defense counsel started recalling people who had already been called in my case.

Defense Calls Its First Witness

On their first day of calling their witnesses, the defense started by recalling a number of the witnesses that we called for our case. The first person was Christa Dubill. She spent a lot of time talking about her upbringing, education, career, and being a public figure working as a television news anchor. I can only assume the defense focused on her meager upbringing to give our working-class jurors something to identify with. Despite being a six-figure earner at KSHB-TV, she made a point to tell the jurors that her father "didn't do anything fancy," and "he just drove a bus" on the Barksdale Air Force Base.

In her recounting of my interactions she witnessed with Melissa Greenstein about the use of file video on a story, she said multiple times that I was angry and raised my voice. At one point, she went even further in saying that there was hand and body motion, and I was leaning into Melissa as I talked about the file video. Then she described Melissa's demeanor as "pleading." So here you have it—the angry black woman attacking the white damsel in distress who is afraid and pleading for reprieve. Wow. I could not believe her vivid descriptions of my angry demeanor and voice as she recounted the exchange in 2019, seeing as in 2015, when she gave the HR director her account of what she saw, it mentioned none of the above.

When my attorney challenged her inconsistency, she said, "I didn't know it would be relevant." From there, she told the jurors about a conversation that she and I had in the bathroom that left our news director, Carrie Hoffman, blotchy and teary-eyed in her office. According to Christa, Carrie had overheard a conversation that Christa and I had about a couple of jailhouse interviews I had done and my frustrations in trying to get approval to do a story on the two black men who believed they were wrongly convicted or had received excessive sentencing. And somehow, Carrie took that conversation to be a violation to the white solidarity that she shared with Christa, so she cried about it and called Christa into her office so Christa could see her cry. Christa told the jurors that Carrie seemed very "distraught," and the conversation with Carrie made her feel like "the blood had rushed out of me." According to the independent investigator, after this bathroom conversation about my jailhouse interviews, Christa said she was "done with Lisa."

I had no idea why she felt like this. I have no choice but to assume that the appearance of a break in their white solidarity would make her feel like she was dying because Christa knew that the appearance of a connection with me would mean she was an enemy of the station, and she could not risk that. Thank God, my attorney challenged her on the cross where she had to admit that despite all the crying among the white managers, she had no reason to believe that I had seen or had knowledge of any of these white women crying about me or over me. This conversation in the bathroom would have happened months before the posting of *The Guardian* article, which made it even clearer to me that her outrage over the article was purely her supporting Carrie and KSHB-TV in helping them to get rid of their problem—me.

In fact, when Carrie, the news director, got back on the stand, she even told the jurors despite recounting the same ridiculous bathroom scene that, "No, Lisa has not seen me cry."

After a lot of back-and-forth with my attorney, Christa had no choice but to admit that. Because of all the crying over me that she was aware of, she erroneously assumed that my posting of the article was a passive-aggressive dig at my white superiors in the newsroom. She told the jurors, "It was possible she was being passive-aggressive posting that article." She went on to explain anyone "connected with her on Facebook could see it, and it's known there's been tension in the newsroom for a long time."

Bingo. My attorney immediately connected her admission of tension in the newsroom to my lawsuit. Again, she tried to fight the connection but had no choice but to admit that the lawsuit that I legally had the right to file against my employer was causing unwanted tension. Tension that seemed to motivate a lot of people to work in solidarity to get rid of me which included calling for my firing for sharing an article about "White Tears."

In talking about her e-mail to the HR manager, Christa repeated several times that she thought the article painted white women in a derogatory way by the color of their skin, which bothered her. Sitting there, listening to her speak, I couldn't help but wonder how she justified the way black people were depicted consistently in the newscasts she anchored. Does it bother her when nonwhite people are depicted in negative lights? Apparently not.

From there, Christa dissected the "White Tears" article, saying the picture of the white woman crying with makeup running down her face on the front of the article was offensive. The mere image of a white woman in distress was offensive? I couldn't help but think about the countless grieving black mothers I'd interviewed and put on television. Did their tears bother you?

During the juror questions, one asked her why she didn't just talk to Lisa about the post. She had already told the jurors that she didn't see me in the newsroom after Jessica McMaster showed her the article on her phone.

Her answer was, "It didn't occur to me to try to call her." So it didn't occur to her to call me, talk to me, or e-mail me about the post. But it did occur to her to call and e-mail human resources and the station's general manager.

The most interesting question that the jurors asked in my opinion was, "Did you want Lisa Benson fired?" Despite the e-mail that she sent to HR to the contrary. She told the jurors, "It was not my goal. Never."

I was encouraged when I heard this and other questions that the jurors asked. It was clear that they too saw a connection between my pending discrimination lawsuit and the decision of my white female coworkers to ban together to get rid of me.

The defense counsel recalled my former general manager, Brian Bracco, and during my attorney's cross, he forced him to admit that despite my internal race complaints to corporate human resources, nothing was done. Exhibit 104 was a document created after I had a conversation with a corporate HR representative on the phone about the differential treatment I was facing and witnessing at KSHB-TV. Bracco told the jurors that my complaints were never communicated to him, and the HR person did not contact him after she created the document.

As I was listening to my attorney and the former general manager go round and round, it was clear that E. W. Scripps did not take discrimination complaints seriously and didn't care about how I felt as an employee. To be honest, I was shocked that he had never seen the complaint, but knowing what I know now, they would have protected him from a conversation about race that would have either angered him or made him feel uncomfortable. I mean, after all, Brian Bracco was hired to save the station from its number four position in the ratings, not to make a black reporter feel valued. From there, my attorney got him to admit to the court that there was no reason that I wasn't a good fit for an anchor position or for the investigative reporter position, which, again, made me smile inside because it further validated that there was nothing wrong with me as a reporter. There was something wrong with a system that would not give qualified black reporters the same opportunities that were available to white employees.

I believed watching him on the stand that this was his first time seeing the document that was dated in May of 2015, which referenced him personally.

He went on to confirm for the jury that Scripps should have in place a system designed to make sure that discrimination complaints are fully and fairly investigated but conceded that he didn't even know about the race discrimination concerns I raised.

In one of the many breaks away from the jurors, the defense counsel tried to argue that the negative comments on TheGuardian.com website should be admissible despite the fact that I had never seen those comments and the fact that no one made a negative remark about the article on my personal Facebook page, where I posted the article. The defense attorney tried to make the point that I should have researched the article and the reader responses before I shared it, and I would have learned that some people didn't like it. Thank goodness, the judge saw the foolishness in that argument. They got to say there were negative comments in open court, but they didn't get to read the comments to the jurors. The judge told the defense counsel, "I just don't think that the sentiments of the author are related to the comments that follow the post. The sentiments of the author are contained in the article itself."

My attorney was quickly running out of time to execute his cross-examination of the defense witnesses, so he started just pounding out the most significant questions before turning the witness back over to the defense. In a few of the cross-examinations, I was concerned that my attorney had not spent enough time dispelling the lies of the defense attorney, but I had to just trust that my legal team had a handle on the time and the proceeding enough to know when it was time to just move on. I felt a little encouraged when at a bench conversation the defense counsel brought up my Facebook post following the first week of trial, the weather, and the electrical issues we had in the courtroom before telling the judge that they wanted an extension of the trial. He suggested that the trial be continued into March or April so that they could put on more evidence.

The judge literally laughed out loud before telling the defense attorney that "under no circumstances is the defendant getting another week."

I was encouraged that we were nearing the end of the trial and in the middle of the defense presenting their witnesses, they were looking for every excuse to start over or get more time. I'm sure part of the motivation was the fact that they were being paid by the hour and e-mail, but nonetheless, I saw promise in their discomfort.

The defense continued to call others back up to the stand and a few new witnesses. I could tell they were trying to get as many black people on the stand as possible to speak on their behalf. They definitely capitalized on a lone black attorney they hired and flew into Kansas City to sit at the defense table despite towering over her and interrupting her to the discomfort of everyone sitting in the courtroom.

In 2017, an Independence, Missouri couple sued KSHB-TV for associating them with a story about a man tricking women into having sex on camera. My attorney fought to have that evidence admitted to show that other reporters and employees have made on-air mistakes that even lead to lawsuits but remained employed by the company. He won that argument; the judge allowed my attorney to bring the case to the court's attention on a limited basis. She agreed that it showed mistakes of other employees in the workplace and how those employees were disciplined.

The court did not allow my attorney to question the assistant news director, Melissa Greenstein, on her decision to wear Indian headdress as part of her Halloween costume one year. The judge decided the information was more prejudicial than probative.

Melissa Greenstein Takes Stand

One person the defense called who did not take the stand previously was Melissa Greenstein, the assistant news director. Her arrogant, coy, and somewhat-cocky demeanor was palatable in the courtroom. After painting herself as a perfect, competent, white damsel in distress for the defense attorney, she coyly tried to avoid answering my attorney's questions and had selective amnesia when recounting her deposition in the case. For instance, in May of 2015, when I was suspended for the file video conversation with her at no point did anyone accuse me of yelling. I was suspended in 2015 for the tone of my voice. When she recounted the exchange before the jurors, she said I was combative, yelling, screaming, and I got in her face. She even went a step forward in her damsel in distress shtick by saying, "I was shaken, and I had never been yelled at like that before." There was clearly a contradiction between what she was saying and what the suspension letter said. I was pretty confident sitting in the court-room the jurors were seeing through her lies.

Melissa was particularly helpful to my case when she lied about witnessing the verbal assaults hurled at black anchor/reporter Dia Wall by her white supervisor, Sam Eaton. Initially, Melissa told the jurors, "I did not hear Sam Eaton respond to Dia." After my attorney reminded her of what her deposition said, she admitted that she saw the exchange but said there was no "cursing or verbal attacking" in her opinion.

By the time Melissa was testifying, both Dia and Sam had agreed that Sam instigated the verbal assault, and it included multiple f-bombs. In fact, Dia, the black female employee who they liked, said it was the worst day of her professional career at KSHB-TV. Despite this information already being in evidence, Melissa told the jurors there was no cursing or verbally attacking. Then she went on to blame Dia for the verbal assault that Sam had already taken responsibility for. Melissa said to the jurors, "Dia did come out and yell at Sam. That's what I saw, and that's what I heard, yes."

When Melissa left the stand, the HR guy, Scott Winkler, went back up followed by another white expert. This woman was an asso-ciate journalism professor who was essentially hired to say I was a bad journalist for sharing an article that white people didn't like. The fact that it was on the site of another credible news organization did not factor into her findings. Despite her using her teaching experience and journalism background to further prove that I had no business sharing an article that put white people in an unfavorable light, the part of her testimony that stood out the most was her compensation.

She told the jurors that she was paid $500 dollars an hour for working on my case and half that for travel. As of my court date, she'd accumulated fifty hours, which means her work hours and travel time were still accumulating. So as of the court date, E. W. Scripps had paid her almost half my annual salary to prove that I shouldn't share stuff white people may not like on social media, and I should know what they do and do not like, seeing as no one actually complained to me or on my Facebook page about the "White Tears" article. Her testimony made it even more clear to me that KSHB-TV's fight in this courtroom was exclusively about continuing to silence me as a woman of color and upholding the systemic racism that built its structure. A structure that protects white people and keeps them in the power position. They didn't want to embrace my appeal for change within the company because that would only empower other people of color to do the same. Because clearly, based on the knowledge and performance of their expert witness, this company had money they were more than willing to waste in their commitment to maintain the status quo. At the end of her testimony, my attorney only had twenty-eight minutes left for the remainder of the trial. So he didn't dispute a lot of her testimony; instead, he doubled down on how much she was being paid to be a cheerleader for KSHB-TV. But throughout her time on the stand, I think she discredited herself in many ways, so I wasn't worried.

The defense called Jessica McMaster back to the stand after their expert. Her testimony mimicked her earlier exchange. This time, the defense counsel showed her résumé tape and one of her Adrian Jones stories, a little boy who was abused by his parents and fed to pigs. During the airing of the story, I had to look away. Despite working on the story myself when it was a day-turn story, Adrian Jones's story was emotionally difficult for me. Not just because of the unspeakable abuse this child endured at the hands of those who should have loved him but because the beautiful brown eyes of that little brown boy reminded me of the two little boys I had at home.

The mommy in me could not hold it together, so I purposely looked away from the monitor until the story was over. I didn't want to sit in the courtroom in a puddle of tears. When I looked over at the jurors, I saw two of the women crying. I knew this was a great maneuver on the defense's part to evoke sympathy from the jurors by pimping the pain and trauma inflicted on this little brown boy one more time.

After the video, Jessica repeated a lot of the stuff she said earlier, but they had her tell the court that she had no resentment toward me because of the trial despite the fact that she'd already testified that we stopped talking after she was deposed in my racial discrimination case. If she didn't resent being dragged into the case, then why did she all of a sudden stop talking to me? It didn't make sense, and despite her teary-eyed display for the jurors, I think they could see that her unbridled offense at the "White Tears" article had everything to do with my race discrimination case against the station. I was further encouraged in my thinking when the jurors only had one question for her, "Did you show the article to anyone besides Christa Dubill?

Her answer, seeing as she had already told the jurors that she relates with people of differing backgrounds and had black friends, was telling. Her answer was, "Oh, no." She then continued to explain to the jurors, "Christa was the only person I walked up to and showed it to that day." Bingo! She was depending solely on her white privilege and solidarity with the main anchor to get this black woman out of the newsroom. Sharing it with a person of color would have evoked dialogue, and she squarely wanted me punished.

Cher Congour—Head on a Stick Chick

Throughout the defense's defense of terminating my contract, there had been an unknown person who allegedly overheard me in the station parking lot when I supposedly threatened violence against my news director, Carrie Hofmann.

Now I finally knew who that person was—Cher Congour Leatherwood. I could not believe my eyes as she approached the stand. I knew that I had never said anything like that, and I didn't understand why Cher would lie on me. We had no ill will toward each other; in fact, outside of this very moment, I would have considered us "friendly" at work. She had white skin, but on more than one occasion, she told me that her mother was Vietnamese. Usually, that acknowledgment on her part would follow our conversations about my different hairstyles. At one point, she had requested my friendship on my personal Facebook page, but I declined it because of her close relationship with Melissa Greenstein and Carrie Hofmann. I didn't want my personal life to become fuel for their afterwork fodder. Sitting at the table, thinking of all these truths as she's running down her work history, it dawned on me that that's why she would be willing to lie on me for no apparent reason. No real gain. It was to protect her proximity to power and privilege. She knew that my black skin would garner no professional favor for her now or in her future career, but her alignment and solidarity with white privilege could and would.

She told the court, "I was outside, and I was standing around a wall, and she had come outside on her phone and was very loud, and yelled, 'I am not going to fucking settle. I want her head on a stake.'" She went on to tell the court that she didn't hear me say a specific name, but she assumed I was talking about either Carrie Hofmann or Melissa Greenstein. She then further explained the made-up scenario, saying she was about thirty feet away from me and was tucked behind a wall. But nonetheless, she assured the jurors she could hear me because I was "extremely angry."

She told the jurors that the first person she told about my alleged angry outburst was none other than Jessica McMaster. Wow! What a coincidence. There are more than one hundred employees at KSHB-TV, and Cher felt a need to run to Jessica McMaster and tell her, "Lisa is really angry today."

After a few more questions by the defense attorney, he wrapped by asking Cher, "Have you stated in the past that you're afraid to be in the same room with Ms. Benson?" She responded by saying, "I had, yes." Here we go again. The angry black woman whom everyone is afraid of. Surely, at this point, the jurors have to be wondering how such a violent angry person could stay employed at the same job for more than fourteen years.

On the cross-examination, my attorney didn't even talk to her about parking lot story, but a juror had a question. "If you were standing around the corner, how do you know it was Lisa without seeing her?" In answering that question, she added another never-heard detail to the parking lot lie, saying, "When I went back inside, I had to walk behind her, and I could recognize her from the back."

As she left the witness stand, I was still blown away, not only by her willingness to lie on me but by the pure stupidity of the lie. I mean, if I were going to plan the beheading of my boss at work, surely, I would have at least walked to the back of the parking lot by the fence line or sat inside of my car. I mean, everyone knows secrecy is an important factor in any well or poorly planned attack or crime. Surely, I wouldn't be angrily screaming my plans for a violent attack at the back door of my job in the middle of the workday.

Geez, I was optimistic that the jurors could see through her lies, but this honestly did a number on me regarding my trust of women. How could a woman who had no dog in this fight be willing to lie and throw me under the bus? Thanks to my research and dig for knowledge and understanding throughout this entire ordeal, I knew that despite having a Vietnamese mother, her white skin, white father, and white husband put her in close enough proximity to power, that she would be willing to lie to maintain favor in their eyes. So despite our jovial, culturally exposed conversations, I was expendable. Her relationship with these white women was not.

Cher proved this to me shortly after the trial was over by being one of the first former coworkers to reach out to me. She texted me a screengrab that included a picture about the verdict from *KC Call* newspaper. I responded by telling her that she'd clearly sent this to the wrong person. She had the nerve to text me, "I meant to send a text with it. Lol," followed by "I was gonna tell you that I hope that your ok and I'm glad your speaking out!"

This kind, supportive text message from a woman who testified in federal court that she was afraid of me. So…I responded saying, "Oh…considering you told a federal judge and a jury of eight that you were afraid of me & I wanted Carrie's head on a stick. I assumed that this text was for someone else. Take care."

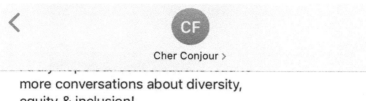

Cher Conjour >

more conversations about diversity, equity & inclusion!

👍 8   1 Share

👍 Like   💬 Comment   ↗ Share

Hi, I think you may have accidentally sent me a screen grab of my own post. ~Lisa B.

No actually I meant to send a text with it. Lol. I was gonna tell you that I hope your ok and I'm glad your speaking out! I was also wondering if your KCUR interview will be online. I'd like to listen.

Oh...considering you told a federal judge and a jury of eight that you were afraid of me & "I wanted Carrie's head on a stick" I assumed that this text was for someone else. Take care.

Delivered

       iMessage

I didn't hear from her again. Her friendly text after her blatant lie further proved to me that I was foolish my entire life. I was foolish to believe that just because I talked like them, dressed like them, worked with them, and even allowed our children to play together didn't mean these privileged white-skinned people could see me. They saw the performance I put forth each day to center and assimilate to whiteness. But the truth is, they knew just like I knew and tried to ignore that every day I show up in white spaces as a black woman, my blackness showed up before my womanhood. It always has and always will. And every "white-skinned" woman who took the stand to hurl lies about me knew that just like the words of Ruby Hamad's article, "The legitimate grievances of brown and black women are no match for the accusations of a white damsel in distress…whose innocence is taken for granted."

These women were liars. But they knew that my black skin had already painted me as the aggressor when they had no proof of the charge. I also knew that in highlighting the role that white women play in supporting systemic racism, I wasn't going to gain support from the four white women on the jury. At this point, I felt my only hope was in the four men on the jury panel and their willingness to fight for me.

The defense called the so-called independent investigator, station leadership, and corporate leadership to the stand to go over facts, exhibits, and testimony that the jurors had now heard several times. And finally, after more legal maneuvering by defense counsel, it was time for jury instructions. I was extremely anxious when the defense rested its case, but after nine full days of testimony, I was ready for my case against E. W. Scripps to be over and for the next chapter of my journey to begin.

Christa Dubill Promoted to Main Anchor, Again

In the midst of writing this book, I received an e-mail on April 11, 2019, from my attorney. It contained a link to a Tony's KC blog post, entitled, "KSHB-TV dumps married couple and announces newsies Christa Dubill and Kevin Holmes as evening anchors."

I could feel the disappointment, frustration, and hopelessness rumbling up the pit of my being. How could they do this? Why would they do this? I won the retaliation portion of the lawsuit. The jurors ruled that they had wronged me in firing me for sharing an article about institutionalized racism. Christa was the anchor who reported the article to HR and demanded that this was a "fireable offense." How is she now being promoted and rewarded for helping to get rid of me? Ironically, I spent the night before reading articles and Instagram posts by Rachel Cargle. Cargle is a young black anti-racism advocate. I had recently missed her visit to Kansas City but watched her hold her own at the *Red Table* with Jada Pinkett Smith. Watching her defend her anti-racism activism, I'd already decided that I needed to start showcasing the willful ignorance that dominated the defense counsel's case and the employees who did and still benefit from its operations and hiring practices that are stoked in white supremacy. So now, I was ready to "Rachel Cargle" their asses with truth bombs on Instagram and Facebook.

I showed the article to my husband as we hurried to get the boys dressed and off to school and childcare. After drop off, I told my husband I wanted to say something. I wanted to do something. I wanted to respond to this slap in the face on social media. My husband and closest friends convinced me to calm down and at least run it past my attorney. I sent him an e-mail, informing him that I wanted to say something publicly on social media. I then forwarded the link to several friends, other black journalists, fellow anti-racism advocates, and my sisters.

The reactions via text message ranged from "Black women in white spaces stand no chance when stuff like this is allowed to happen, from the top down" and "It's disgusting" to "This is ridiculous."

I agreed with every supportive comment but started to question if all this fighting, anti-racism training, and teaching even mattered. Not only did we win in federal court for retaliation, we also showcased the racial disparities that exist in that newsroom. Nonetheless, nothing had changed. In fact, the woman who was so racially ignorant that she helped lead the charge for my firing for merely sharing an article on racism had now been promoted to the primary main anchor position—a position she held previously. She was demoted from the main anchor job in 2015 because as Brian Bracco put it, "We were number four in the ratings" when she was the primary female anchor. At the time, Christa told a local magazine, "My youngest is starting school this fall. I couldn't keep working the late news." At the time, as an employee at the station, I knew there was some media spin on her obvious demotion from the prime time news slot. But honestly, I am a bit surprised that she has forfeited home and family time to get back behind the anchor desk at ten o'clock at night. But I say that never earning her more than $200,000 a year salary or the lifestyle that salary affords.

I so desperately wanted to write an open letter to KSHB-TV and Christa Dubill to highlight the white privilege, white solidarity, and institutionalized racism that would reward her with this position with not so much as diversity training for anyone at the station. I wanted to sound off on Facebook and Instagram, showcasing my disappointment and disgust over the station's decision. Despite the lawsuits, trial, and negative publicity, they didn't decide they needed to do anything to raise racial awareness or knowledge within the company or in the KSHB-TV newsroom. What about Dia Wall? She is a black weekend anchor whom you like. What about Dee Jackson? He too filed a race discrimination lawsuit against the station while still on payroll. Is he making it up too? Why promote Christa Dubill back into a position where she had already been demoted from?

I got an e-mail notification. It was my attorney encouraging me to hold my social media response to Christa's promotion until after the evidentiary hearing that he was still working on. In addition to still fighting KSHB-TV in my case, he was also working for future relief for me, essentially more than the $200,000 awarded by the jurors to make up for lost income. Despite my disappointment, I followed his advice. I felt so defeated, but at this point, I didn't want to do anything to compromise their financial recovery or mine.

After sitting in my car, questioning if I had made the impact I'd hoped for in 2015 when I filed my initial grievance, I got a call from Kevin Holmes, the new black male prime time ten o'clock anchor. The first in KSHB-TV's history. I'd called him earlier to congratulate him. But honestly, I questioned if he'd call me back. At this point, I felt like a deadly virus to my former coworkers. Only a couple were still talking to me. I heard his robust voice on the phone followed by a funny story and couldn't help but laugh. At the first break in his conversation, I congratulated him on his promotion to main anchor. He responded with a huge "thank you" followed by an "I appreciate you." Kevin and I had run into one another at a *White Fragility* book discussion after my termination. So I knew he could see what I saw in that newsroom. I only hoped that he used that knowledge to negotiation his contract and his pay with KSHB-TV. Something about the energy and excitement he exuded in our brief conversation assured me that he had.

We recapped the historical context of being the first black male prime time anchor at the station, and then the conversation quickly moved onto details and start dates. But his acknowledgment that my story at KSHB-TV had positively affected him somehow calmed the frustration and hopelessness brewing in my gut. We exchanged a number of pleasantries before ending the call.

I got a few phone calls from friends who were shocked and saddened by the news and wanted to check on me. Thanks to supportive friends and my conversation with Kevin, I felt a little more empowered that my lawsuit and battle in court did have a positive impact. Even if that impact was not manifesting itself as changes in the white solidarity that exits among leadership or the company's acknowledgment that it needs to undergo company-wide anti-racism, diversity, and inclusion training, I felt a little more hopeful. By midmorning, I had packed up my laptop and headed to a local bakery to continue writing my book.

Closing Arguments

In closing arguments, my attorney reminded the jurors that they were upholding laws that protected all of us in the workplace from retaliation and discrimination. I thought this was a great final attempt to appeal to our working-class jurors. He went on to remind the jurors that we were here because this company fired a person who dared to speak out, sue the company, and stay around, as is her lawful right. One of the more powerful statements he made during closing arguments was, "If your system of justice can't work for the Lisa Benson's of the world, it can't work for anyone because it's too hard to stand up against a powerful corporation. That's how important your job is today."

Dennis continued to use his decades of experience and charisma to quickly remind the jurors of the evidence and remind them of their civic and moral duty to uphold justice.

My attorney made me feel both proud and vindicated when he told the jurors, "Today, February 8, 2019, is the end of a journey that Lisa had to make. Someone who knew she had to fight a major corporation, willing to say and do anything to besmirch her character."

He reminded the jurors of the defense's failed attempts to show them a false picture and portray everything to fit a false narrative about who I was as a black woman.

I truly hoped that the jurors got that too. My fight wasn't just for me. It was for so many other voiceless people who have already been discounted for their gender or the color of their skin. In his final appeal to the jurors, my attorney quoted Dr. Martin Luther King, saying, "Ladies and gentlemen, Martin Luther King said that injustice anywhere is a blow to justice everywhere. And he's right. The simple truth is here, Scripps has a system failure that ruined Lisa Benson's career."

His closing was poignant and hard hitting. If I'd had one black person in the jury, I would have expected a swift victory. But the absence of a true jury of my peers left me amazed by my attorney's delivery, poise, and confidence but still 100 percent unsure of the outcome.

The defense attorney took over after my attorney summarized my case for about forty-five minutes. In their closing arguments, they continued painting me as an angry violent woman who was incompetent at her job. They even put up a misleading exhibit to make it appear as though I didn't even apply for the positions we were litigating over. It was frustrating to listen to, but at this point, I was ready for the jurors to do their job and decide my fate.

CHAPTER 10

The Verdict

The jurors started deliberations at 2:20 p.m. on February 8, 2019. My attorneys were instructed to stay nearby or give the court deputy their cell phone number in the event of a jury question or verdict. Within the first thirty minutes of deliberations, there was a jury question, seeking specific exhibits that were introduced from both our side and the defendant's side. They asked for more than twenty exhibits and my performance review, as well as Jessica McMaster's.

At 4:39 p.m., two hours into deliberations, the jurors asked for exhibit 414, the May 24, 2015, EthicsPoint complaint I filed, documenting racial discrimination. The request for documents continued into the evening hours. Deliberations continued for more than six hours, and at 9:34 p.m., the court deputy walked in and said, "I understand we have a verdict."

I was sitting in the gallery with supporters and friends talking about a myriad of topics. It took a few seconds for me to realize what she'd said and that this was the moment I'd been waiting for. I looked at Lora McDonald and said, "What do you think?" She looked me squarely in the eyes and said, "I don't know."

Other attorneys who were present to support Dennis went out in the hallway to let him know that the jurors had a verdict. I walked back to the plaintiff's table for the last time to hear the decision of the jurors. The judge also informed the attorneys that the jurors did not want to talk after the verdict was read. My heart sank. I was worried that they had not moved in my favor since they'd already declared they didn't want to talk about the verdict.

As the jurors walked back into the courtroom for the last time, the foreman, a younger white male, had a red blotchy face. He didn't look like he'd been crying or anything, but it was clear that he'd encountered a little stress as he took his seat.

The judge read each verdict form in its entirety before sharing the jurors' decision. The judge said, in verdict form A, on Lisa Benson Cooper's claim against Scripps Media, Inc., that she was denied a promotion to weekend anchor in 2013 based on her race, we find in favor of the defendant. She repeated the almost exact same words for verdict form B regarding the investigative reporter position in 2015. They found in favor of the defendant.

In all honesty, I wasn't surprised based on the defense's maneuvering for the 2013 weekend anchor position. But the idea that Jessica McMaster's nursing experience trumped my actual reporting experience when we both applied for the job in 2015 surprised me.

At this moment, my heart sank. I was zero for two. I thought, "If I lose this thing, I know my personality is not going to let me quit. We're going to have to get them on appeal. Oh no! I want this to be over. I don't want to have to go to an appellate court." My mind was racing. I started to press my fingernails into the palm of my hands to calm my nerves. I continued to look straight ahead at the judge. I didn't want to give anyone at the defense table the satisfaction of my disappointment as I feared that the jurors didn't believe me.

Next up, verdict form C. The judge repeated the same pattern of words as my heart was beating out of my chest. She continued saying, "For retaliation based on her 2015 suspension, we find in favor of the plaintiff. She went on to say the awarded damages were $1,000 and the punitive damages against Scripps were $50,000."

I immediately thought, *Yes!* They believed something I said. I won something. I was elated that this now more than three years' journey did end with a measurable victory. Thank you, God!

The judge continued to read verdict form D, which read, "Retaliation based on the nonrenewal of her contracts, we find in favor of plaintiff." The jurors also decided that my employment would not have ended because of my own misconduct outside of my discrimination case and the company's retaliation. They awarded damages at $25,000 and punitive damages against the Scripps at $125,000.

I immediately knew that the monetary numbers didn't add up to much financially, especially thinking about attorney fees, but I was happy to at least have a victory so I could mentally move on. I turned to my attorney, and Dennis said, "A win is a win," which further validated my feeling. I could not believe that this federal jury of seven white people, including four white women believed unanimously that this black woman had, in fact, been retaliated against. I didn't understand how they could clearly see the retaliation, but they could not see the discrimination, but understanding the cultural climate created by the Donald Trump presidency, I accepted their decision.

The defense counsel decided to poll the jurors, so one by one, each juror had to verbally confirm that this was their collective decision.

I walked into the galley, and my friend Lora McDonald greeted me with tears in her eyes and a big hug. She said, "You did it, girl." I smiled, chatted, and hugged others in the galley before heading back to our little conference room to gather up my things for the last time.

As we walked down the stairs of the courthouse, I looked up at the light to cross the street and saw my husband stopped at the light with my two boys in the car. I walked over to the passenger window and said, "We won the retaliation case. They won the discrimination case." He pumped his fist in the air and screamed, "Yes! We won!" In classic Carl Cooper style, he refused to give any energy to the negative, he'd already moved onto the victory.

The Morning After

The next day, I returned a litany of calls and voice mails that I'd missed during the two-week trial. With the mixed verdict, I could tell that my family and friends didn't know how to feel, so I made it a point to tell people that I was happy with the jurors' decision and elated that this chapter of my life was over. I found that my contentment and joy gave them the permission they needed to breathe a sigh of relief for me and for themselves. They needed to know that I was okay. And I was.

Later that morning, I received a call from my attorney Dennis. He said he wanted to let me know what's going on, and "I want you to understand that we won last night. A win is a win." He went onto explain how the victory in the retaliation made me eligible for front pay, which is essentially money from my former employer to remedy the money I could have made had they not wrongfully terminated. And the defense attorney was responsible for attorney fees. I was elated that my attorney was also going to be paid by my former employer. I know my attorney does well for himself, but it truly mattered to me that this extraordinary attorney, who took my discrimination case, would be compensated for his time and effort in fighting for me. Despite the financial toll of losing my job, for some reason, I was still more worried about my attorney being compensated for believing in me. The rest of the day was spent responding to e-mails and calls. A couple of local radio stations were interested in my story. I received a call from a producer of the *Dr. Phil* show and a reporter with the *New York Times* covered part of the trial, and he was reaching out for an update. I knew that I wanted to get this story out, get my story out, but I really didn't know how to do it the right way. My attorney and I did a couple of radio shows, and a reporter with the *KC Star* requested an interview with Dennis and I about the case. During the interviews, Dennis restricted some of the things he wanted me to say, but I was happy to be able to say the names of the two white women who interjected themselves into my story. I could now speak freely about the two white women who used their position, power, and privilege to get me fired for sharing an article. I knew in my heart of hearts that they did this expecting complete anonymity. They were wrong, and now I was going to take every opportunity to say their names whenever I could because they bullied their way into my discrimination case and changed the entire focus of my lawsuit.

The *KC Call* did an article on my verdict, entitled, "Former Channel 41 Reporter Wins Retaliation Portion of Lawsuit Against News Station." The *KC Star* entitled their article, "Former KSHB

Reporter Lisa Benson Cooper Challenged the System and Won—Sort Of."

Both articles gave a true and fair glimpse into my case, my struggle, and named the two women.

In the *KC Star* article, Toriano Porter wrote, "When African Americans challenge systemic racism the results can be devastating. That has never been more evident to Lisa Benson Cooper, who was fired from her job as a reporter at KSHB-TV Channel 41 for sharing on her personal Facebook page an article on white fragility."

His words read like music to my ears. In the first paragraph, he captured the essence of my entire plight with KSHB-TV. Systemic racism is what allows a tenured black female reporter to work for a company for more than fourteen years and never be eligible for a promotion. White fragility allows two white women to not like an article that I read and decide that I should be punished for it, and it allows the white male decision-makers to wage their power and authority to grant their wishes.

I was so pleased that the journalist, Toriano Porter captured the complexity and the irony of my case in his article, writing, "Two white colleagues at KSHB, identified as Christa Dubill and Jessica McMaster in court testimony, complained that the Facebook post was hurtful. Company officials deemed it inappropriate, suspending and then ultimately firing the veteran reporter. Conversations about race are inherently difficult. But they are important and necessary. Cooper and other African Americans should not be forced to remain silent about relevant issues in the workplace."

His perfect synopsis of my story truly encouraged me to share it more and to help others understand and see the subtle yet blatant ways in which racism shows up in our everyday spaces disguised as something else. The more people who are willing to learn and talk about systemic racism, unconscious biases, and white fragility, the better off we'll all be as a society.

CONCLUSION

My confusion and quest for knowledge led me to numerous anti-racism discussions, workshops, and book discussions. It also led me to pursue a diversity and inclusion certification through Cornell University. I completed the coursework in December of 2018. I knew that once this entire ordeal was over, I'd want others to benefit from my journey. Since earning my certification, and thanks to amazing friends and mentors, I've started educating others on diversity, inclusion, systemic racism, unconscious biases, and the history of race in America. I've started doing informational sessions and workshops. I share my personal experiences as part of my commitment to help people understand how racism works in today's world and how truth, knowledge, and racial awareness is the antidote.

Moving forward into my next chapter of life, outside of TV news, I hope to have an impact on anti-racism education. Attending sessions on systemic racism and the two-day workshops through the Racial Equity Institute (REI) on the history of race in America forced me to look at myself and my world differently. This new perspective has helped me to heal the hurts of my past career and work toward a world where people will address racial disparities in the workplace because of the trainings that I lead. The world needs to understand that it's not just up to people of color to interrupt and dismantle racism. By spreading racial knowledge and truths, I hope to create co-conspirators in constructing more accepting working and living spaces that acknowledge the racial hierarchies that exist in America. An understanding that will give room for authentic, truth-laden dialogues about the racial inequities that still exist in the framework of this nation. Conversations, knowledge, and education that can lead to real systemic transformations throughout structures and ideologies. As Nelson Mandela so eloquently stated,

"Education is the most powerful weapon which you can use to change the world."

And I agree.

ACKNOWLEDGMENT

I am forever grateful to my husband, sisters, and girlfriends who spoke prayed and prophesied this book into existence.

From the moment I was suspended from KSHB-TV, I was comforted by old friends and soon to be new friends who took powerful steps in helping me understand my present circumstances and prepare for my future. These genuine, brutally honest conversations from amazing women of color gave me the courage to learn, grow, and share my truth, unapologetically.

These powerful women guided me through the strategically aloof waters of my cross-racial relationships amid blatant racism, while elevating my consciousness regarding the elitism that exists within communities of color.

I owe a debt of gratitude to Tiffany Dwight Estell, Mandisa Womack Potter, Chelsea Clark, Dr. Kia Turner, Pakou Her, Stephenie K. Smith, Justice Gatson, and Nicole Jacobs Silvey. From phone conversations and coffees to happy hours, lunches, and reading recommendations—through words and actions you ALL challenged me to show up authentically in every room I enter while validating the power and purpose that exists within me. Thank you!

And of course, I can't celebrate my girlfriends without honoring my very first friends, my sisters Roshon Benson and Norma Benson. Your unconditional love, encouragement, and willingness to read and reread my book meant more than you'll ever know.

I am because you are. I love you both beyond the depth of my words.

Speaking of my book, the data and facts would not be so bountiful without the thorough work of my attorney Dennis Egan and his incredible team at The Popham Law Firm. I'm grateful for access to documents, transcripts, and engaging exhibits. However, I'm most grateful to you Dennis for not only believing my story of racial inequities but for being willing to show up and fight for me. It was an honor to work with you, Dennis.

And last but certainly not least, a great big thank you and a "you were right" to my husband and life partner Carl Cooper, who threatened to write this book for me if I didn't get to work! He was the first person to encourage me to write my story and read the manuscript.

I am forever grateful for your love and unyielding support of my hopes and dreams.

I look forward to living the vision and purpose God has for our family and future.

I love you, Coop!

ABOUT THE AUTHOR

Lisa Benson is a diversity, inclusion and anti-racism consultant, speaker, author, entrepreneur, and Emmy Award-winning journalist.

She has helped countless people understand how racism is built into the structures that define American culture and values.

Lisa wants her knowledge and firsthand experiences to help others navigate systems, institutions, and organizations when it comes to understanding race and racism.